UNIVERSITY OF NORTH CAROLINA
STUDIES IN THE ROMANCE LANGUAGES AND LITERATURES
Number 34

THE "WISDOM" OF PIERRE CHARRON

AN ORIGINAL AND ORTHODOX CODE OF MORALITY

THE "WISDOM" of PIERRE CHARRON

AN ORIGINAL AND ORTHODOX CODE OF MORALITY

BY

JEAN DANIEL CHARRON

CHAPEL HILL

THE UNIVERSITY OF NORTH CAROLINA PRESS

The University of North Carolina Press

Depósito Legal: V. 39 – 1961

Printed in Spain - Talleres Tipográficos de la Editorial Castalia - Valencia, 1960

To
Jessica

Pour donner au portraict de Charron quelque vie,
Et quelque langue aussy, le Peintre ha iceluy
Ioint aux sages discours de sa Philosophie,
Qui le rendent viuant, et qui parlent pour luy.

N.R.I

FOREWORD

Perhaps it would be of interest to the readers of this work if I explain the similarity of names between the author of this work and the author of the *De la Sagesse*. Family tradition has it that Pierre Charron's father, Thibaud, was a younger brother of one of my direct ancestors. *Cadet de famille,* Thibaud had gone to Paris to strike out on his own in the book selling and publishing business.

The Charron family has lived at Ambarès, near Bordeaux, and at Bordeaux, since at least 1450. They were from father to son, *notaire royal,* members of the *Parlement de Bordeaux, procureur du roi,* etc. This could explain in part the presence of Pierre Charron, *Parisien,* in the environment of Bordeaux and why he spent most of his life there and was so reluctant to leave when the bishop of Boulogne wanted him to come north. It should also be noted that in the editions of Pierre Charron's works the name of the author is followed by the word *Parisien*; these works were first published in Bordeaux, and we could interpret this as the care of the author to inform his readers that he belongs to the Charrons of Paris and not of Bordeaux.

I learned that a manuscript of Pierre Charron had been held in the Charron family until 1870. Then, at that time, it was entrusted to the hands of a son-in-law who had enough literary ambition to want to publish it. But shortly after this his wife died and that was the last that was ever heard of this manuscript.

Pierre Charron's lifelong friend, La Rochemaillet, in an "Eloge" dedicated to the author of the *De la Sagesse* mentions that Pierre Charron had left behind a revised and enlarged edition of the *Trois Vérités* with instructions for the Sieur de Camain, Montaigne's brother-in-law and executor of his will, to publish it; this he never did.[1] This could very well be the lost manuscript, and it would

---

[1] Pierre Charron, *De la Sagesse,* Paris: Douceur, 1607. *Eloge* by La Rochemaillet, p. XIII.

be most interesting to find it again, since this third edition would show how closely Pierre Charron intended to tie the *Trois Vérités* to his more recent *De la Sagesse*.

Pierre Charron's critics have always examined the *De la Sagesse* and its author after separating him from his period and environment and placing him where they think he belongs, somewhere in the retinue of Montaigne, just ahead of the erudite *libertins*. In the midst of this odd arrangement Charron the canon and his *Trois Vérités* look rather perplexing, and this is why to the critics' eyes Charron seems an enigma full of "inner contradictions".

This attitude, which has prevailed until the present in the criticism on Charron, is a very unfair and unjust one, and it is my intent to show that the so-called "contradictions" result from the misconceptions of Charron's critics and that responsibility for these contradictions should rest with them. If, for a change, one chooses to replace Pierre Charron where he belongs, in his own environment, in his own period, under the influence of the dramatic climax of an explosive religious and political situation, then another Charron comes into focus. This Charron, free of any contradiction, has indeed quite a majestic stature at the threshold of the *siècle raisonnable*; he is the first to put into practical and teachable use the humanist culture he had inherited from the ancients. Finally, this Charron has told us loudly by his actions, as well as in his prefaces and in his *Petit Traicté de Sagesse* (which the critics have always by-passed or neglected because of the disturbing evidence they contain), the reasons why he is offering his *sagesse humaine* and how his very intentions were sure to be distorted and misrepresented.

The very interesting works of Sabrié and Bonnefon were my main sources; others, consulted less often, are referred to in the footnotes.

As the work *De la Sagesse* is often referred to as *Sagesse* by French scholars, I have taken the same liberty. Two editions of the *Sagesse* have been used for reference and are always referred to with their publication dates: the 1601 and original edition of Bordeaux; and the 1607 edition of Paris, corresponding to the 1604 edition corrected by Pierre Charron in 1603 before he died. It has been necessary to use the two different editions because of some corrections made by Charron in the later edition and because the two prefaces are different.

Because of the similarity of titles of Charron's main work *De la Sagesse* and his smaller pamphlet *Traicté de Sagesse* some confusion exists when referring to one or the other work. The fact that the

De la Sagesse is a "traité de philosophie" and has been called the *Traité de la Sagesse* has made matters more confusing. It is for this reason I suppose, that some authors. Lanson among them (in his *Grande Encyclopedie* article on Pierre Charron), referred to the *Traicté de Sagesse* as *Petit Traicté de Sagesse*; since I often have to quote and discuss past criticism on Pierre Charron. I will do the same here.

Here I would like to express my sincere appreciation to all those who by their help have made this study and its publication possible; special thanks are due to Professors J. C. Lyons and J. E. Keller for their efficient help, to The University of Texas Research Institute for financial assistance, and in particular to Professors Verdun L. Saulnier and Georges-Paul Collet for their suggestions and encouragement.

Sections have appeared in *The French Review*, XXII, 4 February 1959, and in the *Kentucky Foreign Language Quarterly*, IV, 3 October, 1957.

TABLE OF CONTENTS

LIST OF ILLUSTRATIONS

CHAPTER I

INTRODUCTION

Repeating a well known expression, Paul Bonnefon, author of *Montaigne et Ses Amis,* librarian at the Arsenal, said about Pierre Charron "qu'il est plus célèbre que connu, son nom est presque populaire et ses livres restent dédaignés".[1] These words are still true today, but I would add that he is also *méconnu* because the kind of celebrity he has received is undeserved and results mainly from our author being misunderstood and misinterpreted.

When we view in its entirety the course of the literary criticism on Charron, we realise that, more than with most authors, it seems to have evolved under the auspices of some sort of witticism. The Jesuit Father Garasse should bear the responsibility of initiating a chain-reaction of puns where Pierre Charron's *De la Sagesse* is called *le bréviaire des libertins* and its author *folement sage.*[2] A long succession of literary critics borrowed with complacency these epithets and many others from Garasse. Some among them, like the Abbé Brémond, were able to improve on these witticisms and wrote about *La Folle Sagesse,*[3] and some, like Faguet and Guizot, even coined their own, calling Charron "l'herbier de Montaigne",[4] that is to say that Charron's *Sagesse* is nothing but the dried-up collection of Montaigne's thoughts, all well tagged and catalogued.

The last generation of critics was so delighted by this last pun that, as we will see, hardly one of them can refer to Charron with-

---

[1] Paul Bonnefon, *Montaigne et ses Amis,* Vol. II, Paris: Armand Colin, 1898, p. 213.

[2] J. B. Sabrié, *De l'Humanisme au Rationalisme, Pierre Charron 1541-1603, l'Homme, l'Oeuvre, l'Influence,* Paris: Alcan, 1913, p. 465.

[3] Infra, p. 44.

[4] Sabrié, *op. cit.,* p. 1.

out repeating it after his name. However, while we can readily understand that in the polemic writing of the impetuous Garasse such an extensive use of puns is only a relief from vituperation, we are at a loss to see why modern criticism on Charron chose to follow the same pattern.

I believe that Sabrié, the last and best of Charron's critics, was aware of this when, in the opening page of his study on Charron, he quoted Guizot's witty remark with Faguet's habitual comment that any further study of Charron would be futile as it would only be Guizot's pun cleverly diluted. Although Sabrié concurred with Guizot and Faguet, he nevertheless believed that their witticism could hardly replace a serious study of Charron.

Sabrié was only half right here. Pierre Charron deserves to be studied for his own sake, and to be completely fair a critic should apply to himself beforehand Charron's motto, "Je ne scay", and approach a study of the author of the *Sagesse* only after ridding his mind of any preconceived opinion. This Sabrié did not do, and, although his work filled certain lacunae in the history of criticism on Charron, his very excellent study, *De l'Humanisme au Rationalisme,* is (as he intended it to be) a thesis asserting that Charron was, in Guizot's words, "L'Herbier de Montaigne".

For Sabrié and Bonnefon, as for all of the earlier critics and biographers of Charron, the canon of Condom[5] deserved attention because he was the confidant of Montaigne and the continuator of his thought and because a more exhaustive study of Charron would explain the *Essays* better to us. In this, as we have seen, they follow the pattern set by Faguet and Guizot and before them by Sainte-Beuve, who was the first one after the French revolution to revive the criticism of Charron.

Sainte-Beuve had studied Charron, the "second et disciple" of Montaigne because Charron had been neglected, whereas the author of the *Essays,* his friend La Boëtie, and his "fille d'alliance", Made-

[5] A small city of the "departement du Gers" where Charron spent the last three years of his life. He had exchanged his charges of canon and *écolâtre* in the bishopric of Bordeaux for the similar charges in the bishopric of Condom (infra, p. 71) where he would have more time for his literary pursuits. We will see also that Condom was at that time quite an intellectual center (infra, p. 81). Jean Du Chemin, a poet and a humanist was then bishop of Condom. Sixty-nine years later, in 1669, Bossuet added his name to the list of the distinguished bishops of that city. When Pierre Charron died in 1603 he was referred to as the canon of Condom, and ever since this reference has commonly been used by his biographers.

moiselle de Gournay, had been for some time the center of attention.[6] It appears, therefore, that Guizot's witty remark that the *Sagesse* is a collection of dried-up herbs taken from the *Essays*, has, on the whole, been the basis of modern criticism of Charron. But this premise, basic to most of the theories on Charron, has never been established.

We know that Charron was a friend of Montaigne to the degree that the latter bequeathed to him the right to wear his "coat of arms". But in order to deduce from this that Charron was his disciple and followed his philosophy closely we need more definite and tangible proofs. However, it seems that many of Pierre Charron's critics used this, as Sabrié[7] did, as material evidence to prove Charron's intellectual affiliation with Montaigne.

Scholars of the present generation do not agree with the traditional concept of the age of Henry IV and Louis XIII as established by the Lansons and Faguets. They have pointed out that this concept does not represent a true and complete picture of the period. Authors who have until recently been considered negligible have been resurrected and their true importance in the eyes of contemporaries has been established. For instance, various critics and commentators have exploded the notion that Agrippa d'Aubigné[8] or Guillaume du Bartas,[9] to mention only two cases from the same period as Charron, were poor and unsuccessful imitators of the Pléiade and have established them as really original poets of their time.

I want to paint a new picture of Pierre Charron, of the Pierre Charron who existed and made his mark at the turn of the seventeenth century. In the past sixty years, in spite of the progress and discoveries made concerning Charron by Bonnefon and Sabrié, no effort has been made to restore to the author of the *Sagesse* his true stature. This is due in part to the love of classification in this scientific age: of having a major author as a sun and the authors

---

[6] C. A. Sainte-Beuve, *Causeries du Lundi*, Vol. II, Paris: Armand Colin, 1898, p. 213.

[7] Sabrié, *op. cit.*, p. 47. Speaking of this bequest Mr. Sabrié says: "C'était plus qu'une marque d'amitié que Montaigne donnait à Charron en lui permettant de porter ses armes. N'était-ce pas aussi une sorte d'adoption et comme la reconnaissance d'une filiation intellectuelle?"

[8] Jean Plattard, *Une Figure de Premier Plan dans Nos Lettres de la Renaissance, Agrippa d'Aubigné*, Paris: Boivin, 1931.

[9] Urban T. Holmes, John C. Lyons, Robert W. Linker, *Guillaume de Salluste, Seigneur du Bartas*, 3 vols., Chapel Hill: UNC Press, 1935-41.

of second or third magnitude revolving around him in orderly orbits as planets or satellites.

To achieve my purpose, I propose to first give a survey of the criticism of Charron, focusing attention on how he came to be called a disciple of Montaigne. Then, after a brief review of the background of the period and the life and works of the author, I will point out some facts that have been entirely neglected up to now; as, for instance, his role in the counter-reformation in the southwest,[10] his attacks against superstitions and intellectual atheism,[11] his formulating before Pascal an argument against non-believers which is now known as the Pari de Pascal,[12] and his presenting to the public, thirty-four years before Descartes, the first two points of the *Discours de la Méthode* when exposing his philosophy in his *Petit Traicté de Sagesse.*[13]

Charron wrote the *Traicté* a few months before his death, and he meant to make it an abstract of his *De la Sagesse,* a defense answering complaints and objections, a short and general picture of his *sagesse,* and a declaration of his intentions.

Anticipating the attacks of his critics Charron had forewarned his readers that he would be misinterpreted and quoted out of context, as every time he had separated natural philosophy from the revealed religion for a clearer approach to his subject, his adversaries had ignored his intention in order to place his position as a churchman in jeopardy.[14]

In spite of Charron's clear warning, this is still the main argument against him; Pintard, in his *Le Libertinage Erudit,*[15] refers to Charron with his *folle sagesse* as the priest who taught the *libertins* to do without God. This is an unjust accusation, and if the *libertins* used Charron to further their deist aspirations they always quoted him out of context, and Charron told us that they would.

Pintard's comment reflects also a general opinion allowed by modern critics, that is to say, as Sabrié puts it, "La Sagesse ne professe pas formellement le déisme, mais elle en a l'esprit et les tendances".[16] Such an interpretation of the *Sagesse* is an injustice and

---

[10] Infra, p. 64.

[11] Infra, p. 122.

[12] Infra, p. 89.

[13] Pierre Charron, *Traicté de Sagesse,* Dernière edition, Paris: Robert Feugé, 1642.

[14] Infra, p. 103.

[15] René Pintard, *Le Libertinage Erudit,* Paris: Boivin, 1943, p. 61.

[16] Sabrié, *op. cit.,* p. 379.

is the direct consequence of that long-held theory that Charron is the disciple of Montaigne. The words might be different, but the thought has never changed, and it is again in essence Sainte-Beuve's opinion repeated by Bonnefon that pagan by imagination and sceptic by the nature of his mind, Charron's method for *sagesse* uncovers the lead-wire which from the *Essays* and through the *Trois Vérités* leads to the *Sagesse*.[17]

And this is the reason why I believe and will attempt to show that it is necessary to stop seeing in Charron a disciple of Montaigne. To keep this concept, in spite of all the contradictions it creates, modern criticism refuses to listen to our canon and the obvious purpose intended for his *Sagesse*. It is my opinion, and I will develop this in more detail later, that Charron regarded the *Sagesse* as a tool. He was forging this tool to build with it the philosophy he had to offer as a basis for religion; he had become aware that his *Trois Vérités* would never be acceptable to his Protestant opponents unless he found, to begin with, some *terrain d'entente* on which they could meet.

The *De la Sagesse* therefore had to be concerned with the *sagesse humaine* exclusive of the *sagesse divine*, or else it would not offer the common base for mutual understanding with his opponents that he meant it to offer. And Charron says so in his preface:[18] "De cette sagesse divine n'entendons aussi parler icy, elle est en certain sens et measure traitée en ma première vérité et en mes discours de la divinité." The *Trois Vérités* represented the next logical step to be taken in completing the training of the *sage*.

Pierre Charron made his bid evident by placing on the title page of the *De la Sagesse* a picture symbol of true *sagesse* "une belle femme toute nuë".[19] Overwhelmed by her and kept in chains tied

[17] Bonnefon, *op. cit.*, p. 258.

[18] Charron, *Sagesse*, 1607, p. 4.

[19] *Ibid.*, p. XVIII. Charron gives the following description of the picture of the title page:

"Tout au plus haut, & sur l'inscription du livre, la Sagesse est representée par une belle femme toute nuë, sans que ses hontes paroissent, *quasi non essent*, en son simple naturel, *quia puram naturam sequitur*, au visage sain, masle, joyeux, riant; regard fort & magistral; corps droict, les pieds joints sur un Cube, les bras croisez, comme s'embrassant elle mesme, comme se tenant bien à soy, sur soy, en soy, contente du soy: Sur sa teste une couronne de Laurier, & d'Olivier, c'est victoire & paix: un espace ou vuide à l'entour, qui signifie liberté; se regardant dedans un miroüer assez esloginé d"elle, soustenu d"une main sortant d'un nüage, dans la glace duquel paroist une autre femme semblable à elle: Car tousjours elle se regarde & se cognoist.

DE LA
SAGESSE
TROIS LIVRES.
PAR
PIERRE CHARRON
Parisien Docteur
es Droicts.
Troisiesme edition reueüe
et augmentée.
M.DC.VII.

A PARIS.
Chéz Dauid Douceur Libraire Iuré ruë Sainct
Iacques a l'enseigne du Mercure arresté.

Auec Priuilege du Roy.

L. Gaultier fecit.

to her pedestal, we see four women, symbols of the evils of Charron's time, which he felt had to be overcome and kept in check if any mutual understanding between men was ever to be reached.

The two women on the left symbolise mob passion, so easy to excite and unleash, and public opinion, so changing and unreliable. Both of these evils, and we will point these out later, had been the causes of countless excesses on both the Protestant and the Catholic sides during the wars of religion and at the time of the League.

The first of the women on the right symbolises superstition. Charron seems to hate superstition especially, as we will see later. He was aware that superstition was one of the Protestants' grounds of complaint against many Catholics. It is likely that some of the Catholic counter-reform decrees our canon had to enforce dealt with superstition, and let us note here in passing that his feelings towards superstition could not have been inspired by Montaigne's who said this about it: "Toutes belles rêvasseries, qui sont en crédit autour de nous, méritent au moins qu'on les escoute, et qui ne s'y laisse aller, jusques là, tombe à l'avanture au vice de l'opiniastreté pour éviter celui de la superstition."[20]

The last woman symbolises the conceited and *pedantesque* science. Charron did not subscribe to the argumentative "know-it-all" of the old school and he held the opinion that its methods were a stumbling block to mutual understanding.

The interpretation of this symbolic picture from the title page of the *De la Sagesse* gives us the true meaning of Charron's aim. Now, the entirety of Charron's works needs no longer to suggest

---

A son costé droit, ces mots, JE NE SCAY, qui est sa deuise, Et au costé gauche, ces autres mots PAIX ET PEU, qui est la deuise de l'Autheur signifiée par une raue mise en pal, entortillée d'un rameau d'Olivier, & environnée de deux branches de Laurier en Ovale.

"Au dessous, y a quatre petites femmes, laides, chetives, ridées, enchaisnées, & leurs chaisnes se rendent & aboutissent au Cube qui est sous les pieds de la Sagesse, qui les mesprise, condemne & foule aux pieds, desquelles deux sont du costé droit de l'Inscription du livre, scavoir, Passion & Opinion. La Passion, maigre, au visage tout alteré; l'Opinion, aux yeux esgarez, volage, estourdie, soustenuë & par nombre de personnes, c'est le Peuple. Les deux autres sont de l'autre costé de l'inscription; scavoir, superstition au visage transsy, joignant les mains comme une fervante qui tremble de peur; Et la science, vertu ou preud'hommie artificielle, acquise, pedantesque, serve des loix & coustumes au visage enflé, glorieux, arrogant, avec les sourcils relevez, qui lit en un livre, où y a escrit, OUY, NON."

[20] Montaigne, *les Essais,* edited by Villey, Paris: Alcan, 1922, 3 vols.

any psychological contradictions in our canon. The path to the true religion of the third *Vérité* will be opened to the *sage* by the *Sagesse,* and the *Discours Chrétiens* will train him in the Christian virtues. It is difficult to see how Charron could have inherited this plan from the author of the *Essays.*

CHAPTER II

A SURVEY OF CRITICISM ON CHARRON[1]

In the third division of *Les Trois Vérités,*[2] the first work of Pierre Charron ever published, Charron attempted to refute certain statements in the *Traité de l'Eglise*[3] of Duplessis-Mornay about the definition of the true Church. This brought forth immediate rebuttal from two Protestants of La Rochelle and Montauban.[4] It is true that these two pamphlets were more argumentative than critical, but nevertheless they represent the beginning of criticism on Charron.

The polemist from La Rochelle preferred to remain anonymous, but the second was Jean Gardesy, a pastor-author from Montauban. In the manner so typical of the polemists of the period, they preferred vitriolic abuse to logical reasoning. They boasted (even in Latin verse) of their superiority to Charron, and laughed about the fifteen years delay on the part of the Catholics in answering Duplessis-Mornay. They finally thanked Charron for having given to the *Traicté de l'Eglise* a final stamp of approval by attaching so

---

[1] We have drawn largely from J. B. Sabrié, *op. cit.*, in this chapter for the less well-known criticism on Pierre Charron. P. Bonnefon, *op. cit.*, has also furnished valuable information.

[2] Pierre Charron, *Les Trois Vérités Contre les Athées, Idolatres, Juifs, Mahométans, Héretiques et Schismatiques,* Bordeaux: S. Millanges, 1593.

[3] Duplessis-Mornay, *Traicté de l'Eglise,* Londres: 1578.

[4] *Response à un livre nouvellement mis en lumière, intitulé les Trois Vérítéz en la troisiéme partie duquel l'Aucteur maintient que de toutes les parties qui sont en la Chrestienté, la Romaine prétendue Catholique est la seule vraye Eglise contre ceux de l'Eglise Réformée, et particulièrement contre le Traicté de l'Eglise du sieur Duplessis-Mornay,* La Rochelle: Hierosme Haultin, 1594.

Epistola Johannis Gardesii Montalbanensis ad Petrum Charronium Parisiensem, Montalbani: Dionisius Haultinus, 1597.

much importance to it that it required an answer. Charron replied to them in a special preface to the third *Vérité* in his 1595 re-edition. And again in counter-rebuttal, according to Joly,[5] there appeared in Geneva in 1597 a *Défense de la Response Faicte à la Troisième Prétendue Vérité*. Du Jon,[6] in a new refutation published at Leyden in 1599, concluded the series of Protestant criticisms of the *Trois Vérités*. Du Jon's tone was different; he followed the text of the *Trois Vérités* closely, quoting Charron, striving for a friendly comparison of the two doctrines, and wishing that his criticism might be useful in bringing hearts together in charity and minds in enlightenment. From the above, we can see that Pierre Charron was a center of controversy from the day his ideas first appeared in print.

However, it is around Charron's major work, *De la Sagesse*,[7] that the main controversy has centered since the beginning of the seventeenth century. This is why we have to trace in chronological sequence the vicissitudes of opinion about Charron and his ideas from that day down to modern times. For obvious reasons, consideration will be limited to those critics who have shaped the norm of the changing attitudes toward our canon. The concluding item in this survey will be an attempt to evaluate the importance which modern criticism concedes to Charron in the development of rationalism in France.

The *libertins* of the seventeenth century seem to have taken delight in reading *De la Sagesse*, but only because they placed upon it an interpretation quite different from the one which the author had originally intended.

Charron had developed at length the famous Socratic phrase γνωθι σεαυτον : know thyself.[8] In the process of doing so, one has to rid oneself of all superstitions and unfounded beliefs. When treating the subject of *sagesse*, he was treating of man and his behavior. It is usually very difficult to know all sides of man, since man hides so much of his true inner self from others and even

[5] Joly, *Remarques sur le Dictionnarie de Bayle*, Paris: 1748.

[6] Fr. Du Jon, *Amiable confrontation de la simple vérité du Dieu, comprise ès Escritures Saintes, avec les livres de M. Pierre le Charron qui sont intitulés l'un, les Trois Véritéz contre tous les Athées, Idolâtres, Juifs, Mahumétans, Héritiques et Schismatiques, l'autre la Réplique du même auteur sur la réponse faicte à sa troisième Vérité*, Leyde: 1599, 1st ed., and Genève: Pierre de St. André.

[7] Pierre Charron, *De la Sagesse*, Bordeaux: Simon Millanges, 1601.

[8] Jean Charron, "Defense and Illustration of Charron's *Sagesse*", *Kentucky Foreign Language Quarterly*, IV, 3, 1957, p. 123.

from himself. One should examine oneself from within and remember that the wise man does his duty and keeps the laws, not because they are laws, but because of respect for himself. He is above the laws and would behave in the same way even if they did not exist.

In the preface to his *Sagesse* and in the *Petit Traicté de Sagesse*, Pierre Charron repeated several times that his *Sagesse* is concerned only with the pursuit of human *sagesse*; he is not treating here worldly *sagesse*, which is concerned with the means of reaching a successful station in life, nor divine *sagesse*, which he had abundantly treated in the first of his *Trois Vérités* and in his *Discours Chréstiens*.[9] Therefore he is obviously referring to the *morale naturelle* or conscience, which as all Christians believe, is inborn in man and is intended to keep him on the right path without the help of laws. Needless to say *libertins* and so-called *libertins* like Patin, Naudé, and Gassendi or their heirs like Bayle seized upon such passages in the *Sagesse* and lifted them out of context for further reference without ever quoting the strict limitations of the precise frame of the work of our canon. The *libertins* therefore enjoyed reading the *Sagesse* and some made comments about it.

Guy Patin, who, because of an honest lack of vocation, had refused to enter the priesthood and had become a doctor, was also a great bibliophile with a library of 9.000 books. One of his most prized possessions was the *Sagesse* of Charron.

Writing about the publication of the letters of Balzac he said:[10] "This collection will be precious and contribute as much to the renown of France as did the works of our greatest men: Philippe de Commine's *Mémoires*, President de Thou's *Histoire Universelle*, Charron's *Sagesse*, Bodin's *République*, and Lamothe le Vayer's *Oeuvres*."

In the *Naudaeana et Patiniana*[11] Patin explained the reasons for his admiration. Because of his perspicacity, his clairvoyance, his knowledge of man, Charron would have been one of the shrewdest among the legislators if he had been one of them. And Patin calls them: "Les plus fins de tous les hommes". His friend G. Naudé has also complimented the *Sagesse* and its author several times. In his

[9] Pierre Charron, *Sagesse*, 1607, p. 3; *Les Trois Vérités*, p. 3; *Discours Chréstiens*, infra, p. 116.

[10] Sabrié, *op. cit.*, p. 452.

[11] *Ibid.*, p. 452, citing *Naudaeana et Patiniana*, Paris: 1703, p. 98.

Bibliographia politica[12] he mentions the French moralists worthy of attention. They are: Du Vair, Coëffeteau, Montaigne, and Charron. He even places our canon well above Montaigne because the latter, although remarkable for his thought and style, lacks order and clarity. For him Charron is the Socrates of modern times.[13]

In the *Mascurat,*[14] Naudé has Sainte-Ange say that the *Sagesse* of Charron and the *République* of Bodin are the best works in the world. One day, when the Cardinal Bagni asked Mazarin's librarian which, in his opinion, was the best of all books, he answered that after the Bible it was the *Sagesse* of Charron.

Henri de Pibrac had sent to Gassendi, canon at Digne in Provence, a copy of the *Discours Chrétiens* which could not be found in the bookshops of Aix at that time. Speaking of the esteem he knew that Gassendi had for Charron, he said "...ideo mitto tibi Charronis librum, quo continentur *Tractatus Christiani,* quia scio ejus tibi authoris genium et ingenium placere."[15]

The appreciation of Gassendi for the "genius and the talent" of Charron was then known. Thanking De Pibrac in a letter of April 1621, Gassendi says, referring to Charron and his *Sagesse,* it is a good suggestion to take Charron with him to his solitary retreat: "Quel juge plus sûr?"[16] Thus we see that Gassendi held Charron in high esteem. Sabrié[17] maintains that Gassendi classed him with Seneca, Cicero, and Montaigne —or even above them— since his thought is the condensation of their combined ideas.

We have, therefore, established that the erudite *libertins* liked Charron. It is then not amazing to see that the two major adversaries of *libertinage* in France in the seventeenth century, Father Mersenne and Garasse, considered him an archenemy. They had seen instantly how much *libertinage* could profit by the *Sagesse,* particularly when some passages were used out of context, and they believed it necessary to attack Pierre Charron and thus ruin his prestige and authority.

---

[12] G. Naudé, *Bibliographia politica,* Venice: 1633.

[13] Sabrié, *op. cit.,* p. 447.

[14] Henri Busson, *La Pensée Religieuse Française de Charron à Pascal,* Paris: J. Vrin, 1933, p. 182. Busson refers there to *Naudaeana,* p. 3f.

[15] Sabrié, *op. cit.,* p. 446 and p. 448, citing G. Naudé *Le Mascurat ou Jugement de tout ce qui a esté imprimé contre le Cardinal de Mazarin depuis le 6 Janvier jusqu'à la déclaration du 1er Avril 1649,* Paris: p. 289.

[16] Henri Busson, *op. cit.,* p. 182, citing Gassendi, Opera VI, 1-2, 391.

[17] Sabrié, *op. cit.,* p. 447.

For Naudé the *Sagesse* was second only to the Bible,[18] but Father Mersenne placed it next to Machiavelli's *The Prince,*[19] adding however, that although this comparison was a flattering one for the *Sagesse,* it certainly was not a commendation of its morals.

Following the polemic manner so popular in the seventeenth century, Mersenne begins by saying that Charron's friends as well as his morals are unworthy of a priest.[20] Then he states that the *Discours Chrétiens* are full of dangerous maxims and that the *première vérité* of the *Trois Vérités* is almost heretical. He asserts that the *Sagesse* is Charron's most deadly sin and a great source of evil influence, and if it is not, as some call it, a manual of irreligion, it represents at least a great danger to faith and religion. Charron cannot be forgiven for having remained so equivocal on so many religious points and for not having worried about the false interpretations sure to follow.[21] He should have written the *Sagesse* in a more Christian and religious way. The *Sagesse* is so much the opposite of the ideal of Father Mersenne that he thinks it should be done over.[22] It is too bad that he has so little time, otherwise he would have tried to compose a synthesis of human and Christian wisdom. Then, without incrimination of the intentions of our *théologal* of Condom, he brands the *Sagesse* as dangerous reading for the *libertins* and the deists although a strong and well balanced mind could profit by it. The final words of criticism are even kind. The author of the *Sagesse* had good sentiments, and his last will and testament and the corrections made in the second edition of the book show it.

Sabrié thinks that Mersenne's criticism is "firm, precise and as farsighted as exempt from passion. Its sureness and impartiality are to the honor of the author of the *Impiété des Déistes.*"[23] But Father Mersenne, like his fardistant followers, never tried to see and understand why Pierre Charron wrote the *Sagesse.*

---

[18] Supra, p. 26.

[19] P. Mersenne, *L'Impiété des Deistes, Athées èt Libertins de ce temps, combatue et renversée de poinct en poinct par raisons tirées de la Philosophie et dė la Theologie, ensemble la réfutation du Poème des Déistes,* Paris: Billaine, 1642, p. 228.

[20] Sabrié, *op. cit.,* p. 455.

[21] Pierre Charron did. This is one of the reasons why he wrote the *Petit Traicté de Sagesse.* Infra, p. 103.

[22] Sabrié, *op. cit.,* p. 457.

[23] *Ibid.,* p. 459.

The Jesuit father Garasse[24] was much less moderate than Father Mersenne in his criticism of Charron. According to him, the *Sagesse* is among, "Les livres cabalistiques des nouveaux dogmatisants: les beaux esprits".

In 1624, Garasse published his *Doctrine Curieuse*,[25] which up to now has been his main title to fame. Although his picture of seventeenth century *libertinage* is somewhat similar to Mersenne's, his colorful style and his excited and violent tone had a great popular appeal. Garasse saw two kinds of *libertins:* the kind that leads an uninhibited life void of all moral restrictions; and the kind who add to that same *modus vivendi* the open avowal of atheistic and impious theories. Both, according to Garasse, are thoroughly familiar with the path leading to taverns and with the handling of bottles.

Garasse's intent in the *Doctrine Curieuse* was to inflict a social stigma upon the *libertins* by accusing them of vices scorned by society. He pretended that a bottle was their emblem and that they should be pictured as cutthroats and gypsies, although, he says, the comparison would be unfair to the latter. To write about the *libertins'* doctrines is difficult because in doing so you run the risk of teaching their vicious theories, and "white paper would blush" under your writing. This last expression approaches the *precieux* mannerisms which Garasse often criticised himself. At the end of the work the Jesuit father reproaches the *libertins* for their aristocratic pretensions when they pretend that the masses could not understand their philosophy. Under attack also is the *libertins'* condemnation of all the superstitious devices and beliefs so dear to the average seventeenth-century man, their love and respect for nature. As we will see later, Charron's *Sagesse* is concerned with some of these points, although he always seems to call his reader's attention to these matters only to rid those seeking wisdom of the kind of faults which invite criticism from non Catholics. But in doing so our canon had invited Father Garasse's criticism.

In the usual style of the *Doctrine Curieuse,* Garasse opened his attack on Pierre Charron by making puns on the name of the author of the *Sagesse* and on old wheels.[26] Garasse states that Charron's books are venom disguised as honey but that under the close scrutiny

---

[24] *Ibid.,* p. 459.

[25] P. Garasse, *La Doctrine Curieuse des beaux esprits de ce temps ou pretendus tels contenant plusieurs maximes pernicieuses à la religion de l'Estat et aux bonnes moeurs,* Paris: 1624.

[26] A "charron" in French is a wheel maker.

of a good mind they fall to pieces like an old wheel falling apart, and that the so-called "beaux esprits" absorb the poison without fail and for them it is their kind of *Introduction à la vie dévote.*[27]

But the foregoing is mild in comparison to the ferocious attacks which were to follow in the *Somme Théologique.*[28] This work was concerned almost exclusively with Charron and his *Sagesse.*

Prior Ogier[29] had dared to defend the Canon of Condom and had attacked Garasse. The firey-tempered Jesuit refuted him unequivocally: Pierre Charron was the spokesman for the atheists and *libertins* who hid themselves like the stars of the galaxy which disappear into nothingness because of their smallness. He said he had read and understood Charron. Sabrié agrees that, at most, he had done the first.[30]

Although the Jesuit claims that he is attacking the doctrine and not the author, he calls him a "toucan": a bird from Peru which is nothing but "bec et plume",[31] and, although Charron is a churchman by profession, he is "cynique d'humeur, libertin de religion et prostitué de langue".

In the mind of Garasse, the *Discours Chrétiens*[32] and the *Trois Vérités* are almost as evil as the *Sagesse.* He calls the style of Charron "monstres ou prodiges de discours" and concludes "voilà en peu de mots la *Sagesse,* les *Vérités* et les *Discours Crestiens* de cet escrivain très dangereux".[33]

Finally Garasse ends his criticism, if we can call it that, by stating that Charron must have been hired by Julian the Apostate himself to destroy by the pen what he couldn't stop by the sword. Hence, Garasse felt that he was obliged in conscience to expose the treason of such a man.[34]

---

[27] St. François de Sales, *Introduction à la vie dévote* sold more copies than any other work in the XVIIth century in France.

[28] P. Garasse, *La Somme Théologique des Véritez Capitales de la Rėligion Chrestienne,* Paris: 1625.

[29] Fr. Ogier, *Jugement et censure du livre de la Doctrinė Curieuse de Fr. Garasse,* Paris: 1623.

[30] Sabrié, *op. cit.,* p. 467.

[31] Sabrié, *op. cit.,* p. 460.

[32] Pierre Charron, *L'Octave contenant huict discours du S. Sacrement, avec un autre discours de la communion des Saints,* Bordeaux: S. Millanges, 1600; *Discours Chrestiens, seconde partie,* Bordeaux: S. Millanges, 1601.

[33] Sabrié, *op. cit.,* p. 468.

[34] *Ibid.,* p. 470.

This accusation of treason is the crowning insult against Charron. In the eyes of Garasse he is worse than any savage cannibal, and even prostitutes would not dare to speak as Charron had written.[35]

Garasse's criticism is therefore much more a collection of insults than reasonable accusations, but it is important because, along with similar attacks on Charron by Father Mersenne, it largely charted the course which has been followed by critics of Charron from that day down to recent times. This underlying base is founded on prejudice rather than fact, and hence the prevailing criticism of Charron places him and the intent of his work in a completely false light.

However Garasse's attacks were not accepted by all contemporaries. Saint-Cyran,[36] for example, declared flatly that the *Somme Théologique* of François Garasse should be condemned because it held "Plusieurs propositions hérétiques, erronées, scandaleuses, téméraires et des bouffonneries sans nombre qui sont indignes d'estre escrites et leues par des Chrestiens et des Theologiens". The head of the French Jansenists prides himself on his ability to distinguish between a man and his works and he states that with necessary discretion one can criticise and condemn a doctrine without slander to the author.[37] St. Cyran says that he had never heard of Charron when he read Garasse's work and he believed Garasse was placing the *Sagesse* among the worst books of a deist's library. Then he read the *Sagesse* and was much surprised by the lack of good faith shown by Garasse in his attack.

Very methodically and in great detail Saint-Cyran follows Garasse step by step and corrects his errors (as he saw them) and misinterpretations with the sure hand of a trained theologian. He shows how unjust Garasse had been to Charron in quoting out of context. Garasse had quoted: "Quand on veut discourir des jugements de Dieu, on y trouve à chaque pas des absurditez, dissonances, injustices..." and was careful to omit the following line, "Les Jugements de Dieu sont merveilleux, très difficiles à entendre".[38]

---

[35] *Ibid.*, p. 467.

[36] *La Somme des fautes et faussetez capitales contennuës en la Somme Théologique du Père Fr. Garasse, de la Compagnie de Jésus*, Paris: Joseph Bouillerot, 1626.

[37] Sabrié, *op. cit.*, p. 474, and Sainte-Beuve, *Port Royal*, Tome 1er, Paris: Hachette, 1901, pp. 310-314.

[38] Sabrié, *op. cit.*, p. 476, citing St. Cyran, *La Somme des Fautes et Faussetez*, p. 400.

The bad faith of the Jesuit is evident here because the incomplete quotation makes it appear that Charron was criticizing divine decisions. Actually, as we have just read it, the complete quotation reveals that Charron was trying to prevent his fellowmen from doing that very thing. Charron was well aware that one of the main reasons for the great progress of Protestantism was the opportunity it gave for self-justification by means of individual interpretation of the words of God in the Bible. Charron even foresaw, as we will show later, that this temerity in investigating and interpreting certain mysteries of revelation might lead to an irreligious state of mind. This state of mind, which he calls blasphemous, certainly resembles the intellectual *libertinage* opposed by the Garasses and the Mersennes. Saint-Cyran should have told Garasse that obviously Charron sided with him (Garasse) and that it was Garasse and not Charron who was irreligious. Garasse was condemning Charron for warning his fellowmen to beware of interpreting revelation, a process which had led so many toward the path of self-justification and Protestantism.

Therefore Saint-Cyran has proved Garasse's accusations against Charron to be calumny, although he is not willing to endorse all of Charron's ideas and wishes that he had been more discreet and orthodox in certain of his statements.

Along with St. Cyran, although not sharing the same philosophy, the young Prior Ogier rose to the defense of the *théologal* of Condom. Quite an accomplished preacher himself, author of the official eulogy on the occasion of King Louis XIII's death. Ogier's voice is not to be neglected. Using language worthy of Garasse himself, Ogier calls him a disgrace to the Company of Jesus and unworthy to wear the cloth.[39] Men like Garasse, he said, do a great disservice to religion by defending it in ways more suited to satiric poets and jesters. It is because Garasse is a jester, a buffoon, and a clown that he hates the wise Charron, who always writes seriously with the dignified tone of a scholar. And, furthermore, Charron is the declared enemy of the vain, inept, censoring *pédant,* and Garasse fits that description entirely.[40] Ogier concludes by saying that Charron deserves praise for his talents and his philosophic doctrine.

---

[39] Fr. Ogier, *Jugement et censure du livre de la Doctrine Curieuse de François Garasse,* Paris: 1623.

[40] Sabrié, *op. cit.,* 483ff.

Ogier, a Parisian himself, wants to restore to his proper place another Parisian who can but reflect credit on that great city.

In the middle of the seventeenth century Charles Sorel, who takes great pride in being unbiased and in not propounding any fixed critical program, sums up contemporary opinion about Charron.[41] After citing some of the *Sagesse's* passionate detractors and ardent admirers, he notes that Montaigne enthusiasts consider Charron inferior to him and "qu'il n'est que son petit disciple, et qu'encore qu'il ait mis quelque ordre dans ses ouvrages, cette observation de rhetorique facile aux gens de collège, ne vaut pas l'agreable mélange de son maistre".[42] This point is a very important one for us since it is the first mention in literary criticism of the idea so current today: "Charron, disciple de Montaigne". Sorel adds that some also think that Charron is more dangerous than Montaigne because he wrote as a churchman and not as a layman.

Sorel concludes his commentary on Charron with a moderate defense of our canon. Sorel was a true intellectual. He published his works without offering them in homage to the powerful protectors from whom most seventeenth-century authors generally derived monetary reward and political backing in securing a place on the pension roll. From his novels (*L'Histoire Comique de Francion* and *Polyandre*, for instance), we receive a true picture of different typical characters of his time whose originals can often be identified. His *Bibliothèque Françoise* and his novels have always been a reliable source of exact information on the period for most commentators on the seventeenth century,[43] and no one can have doubts about his stand on superstitions, false devotion and the intricacies of theological controversy. This intellectual attitude of Sorel seems to match Charron's very well, as we will see later.[44]

But keeping in mind the portrait of a Sorel which Adam[45] has given us, "...ni bigot, ni Mazarin, ni Condé", quiet, always careful to avoid formulating a definite opinion by often contradicting himself, we are fully aware that Sorel wants to keep to the middle of

---

[41] M. C. Sorel, *La bibliothèque françoise de M. C. Sorel ou le choix et l'examen des livres françois qui traitent de l'éloquence de la Philosophie, de la Dévotion et de la Conduite des Moeurs,* Paris: 1664, pp. 79 ff.

[42] *Ibid.*, p. 79.

[43] For instance in Antoine Adam, *Histoire de la Littérature Française au XVIIe Siècle,* Paris: Domat, 1948, Vols I, II, we find no less than sixty-three references to Sorel in addition to the pages concerning his works.

[44] Infra, p. 122.

[45] Adam, *op. cit.*, p. 143.

the road. Therefore, conceding that Charron did draw heavily on the ideas of Montaigne and Du Vair, [46] Sorel reminds his readers that Charron rearranged those ideas in orderly sequence and added many subtleties, modifications and opinions of his own. Sorel hopes that his conciliatory position will not result in offending both the supporters and the critics of the *Sagesse*. There is the danger that those who approve of the work may be indignant that he found any flaws in it at all, whereas those who condemn the work may be unwilling to admit any of the good things he found in it. Sorel insists, however, that the unprejudiced reader can benefit greatly by the reading of the *Sagesse*. In this connection Sorel is in accord with the author of the *Sagesse* himself who told us specifically in his *Petit Traicté de Sagesse*[47] that his *Sagesse* is written for the "sage" with an understanding and open mind and not for the "pédant" stuffed with rash preconceived authoritative judgment. In summary, Sorel reminds his readers that Charron has been held in high esteem by many worthy contemporaries well-known for their own probity and integrity, that he had held many positions of confidence and trust in the service of the Church, and that his personal career had not been besmirched by the slightest breath of scandal. Surely such an individual could not have intended to give comfort to the *libertins* nor to undermine the doctrine of the Church![48]

Another elegant and delicate adept of the so-called "libertinage intellectuel", Saint-Evremond, who spent most of his life in England, is shown by Sabrié to be indebted to Pierre Charron.[49] I have checked through Saint-Evremond's works and although he frequently mentions Montaigne's *Essays* and the very special pleasure produced by reading them, he never mentions Charron.

Sabrié feels that Saint-Evremond's scepticism and philosophy parallel Charron's closely and that, like the author of the *Sagesse*, he would have preferred a religion with fewer ceremonies and exterior manifestations and would have liked to live according to nature. This is also the opinion of an editor of Saint-Evremond, V. Giraud, who sees three links in the chain of scepticism bridging the seventeenth century: Charron, La Mothe le Vayer, and Saint-Evremond, who hold to the wise mean between the intolerant

[46] *Ibid.*, p. 76.
[47] J. D. Charron, *Kentucky F. L.*, p. 125.
[48] Sorel, *op. cit.*, p. 82.
[49] Sabrié, *op. cit.*, p. 449ff.

Catholics and the fanatic Protestants and between the Jansenists and the Jesuits.[50]

Saint-Evremond says that he owes his intellectual attitude to Gassendi. It seems therefore strange to us that through such a great and openly admitted admirer of Charron like Gassendi he wouldn't have become interested in the *Sagesse*.

From seventeenth century criticism, we must also mention a passage from a letter of Madame de Sévigné,[51] who writing to her daughter, advises against letting her granddaughter read Montaigne or Charron as fitting material for a moral education.

Pierre Bayle, bridging the seventeenth and the eighteenth centuries in his *Dictionnaire Historique et Critique*,[52] gives us the main critical opinion about Charron in the century of the *philosophes*. Coming as he does at the end of the chain of the seventeenth century intellectual *libertinage*, we can expect from him a very favorable attitude. Bayle agrees with our canon that an understanding of the *Sagesse* requires above-average ability and an elevated mind free of prejudice. In his praise of Charron's doctrine Bayle uses the same system of quoting out of context that Garasse did, but with a very different purpose. The things in Charron's doctrine which Garasse condemned are the very ones which Bayle approves and admires. Needless to say, as we will see later in Charron's own words in the *Petit Traicté de Sagesse*, our canon would have rejected the basis on which Bayle praised him just as quickly as he would have rejected the basis on which Garasse condemned him.

Bayle is delighted to see that Charron recognized a great degree of fortitude of character in the atheist. And the success of the *Sagesse* at this time is an indication of the freedom of thought which was then in the course of development. According to Bayle, France should be proud to have permitted the publication of this work; in spite of the tyrannical opposition of some people, philosophical freedom thus came into being. For Bayle, Charron the philosopher is also a good Catholic and a man above reproach, under a double halo of tolerance and staunch Christianity.

---

[50] *Ibid.*, p. 503.

[51] M. Monmerqué, *Lettres de Madame de Sévigné*, Paris: Hachette, 1862, Vol. IX, p. 413.

[52] Pierre Bayle, *Dictionnaire Historique et Critique*, La Haye: 1737, Vol. IV, pp. 142 ff.

In the same century two men of the Church, a Chartreux and a Jesuit, have something to say about the *Sagesse*. The Carthusian,[53] in a work on the distinction between good and evil, discusses Charron's and Montaigne's attitudes on this matter and accuses them of "relativism". But Charron is by far the more dangerous of the two because of his moral system in which nature is used as a criterion for measuring virtue. Dom Gaudin is not violent; he is, however, alarmed to see that Charron does not use religion as the foundation of his moral system. He didn't realise that in several editions of the *Trois Vérités* our canon had already laid that foundation and that the human morality of the *Sagesse* was only a preliminary step leading the reader to the acceptance of the *Trois Vérités* as the unavoidable conclusion.

The Jesuit, Father Buffier, in his *Cours de Sciences*,[54] far from adopting the attitude of his *confrère* Garasse (they both belonged to the same order), praises the *Sagesse* as an excellent manual of morality. In Buffier's opinion the thoughts that Charron expressed in the *Sagesse* are so deep that they invite reflection, as Charron makes his reader think beneath the surface of what he says. But he also has some criticism: Charron's stoicism is not a sufficient consolation, and his human morality, independent of divine law, is the main cause of the opposition encountered by the *Sagesse*. However, the Jesuit understood that the canon always maintained that true probity and religion are inseparable, but the sceptics deliberately disregarded that aspect of his thought and made Charron one of their authorities.

The seventeenth-century historians of literature and philosophy were in general very kind to Charron.[55] In a history of philosophy since the Renaissance Brucher[56] cites him in company with Vives, Ramus, and Pico della Mirandola. He accuses him anew of having ploughed with the calf (and not the ox) of his friend Montaigne,

---

[53] Sabrié, *op. cit.*, p. 454 citing Dom Alexis Gaudin, *La Distinction et la nature du bien et du mal, traité où l'on combat l'erreur des Manichéens, les sentimens de Montaigne et Charron et ceux de M. Bayle*, Paris: Claude Allier, 1704, Ch. II.

[54] Sabrié, *op. ct.*, p. 527, citing P. Buffier, *Cours de Sciences sur des principes nouveaux et simples pour former le langage, l'esprit et le coeur dans l'usage ordinaire de la vie*, Paris: 1632.

[55] Sabrié, *op. cit.*, p. 526 ff.

[56] Jacobi Bruckeri, *Historia critica philosophiae a tempore resuscitatarum in occidente litterorum ad nostra tempora*, Lipsiae: 1742-1744, vol. IV, part. I.

but agrees, nevertheless, that our canon showed deep insight into human nature.[57]

J. F. Reimann[58] mentions him also in his history of atheism. As Sabrié notes, it is a strange place in which to find a canon and a professor of theology. But he is in good company there, for although we find there the names of Rabelais, Bayle, Dolet, Bonaventure des Périers, and Bodin, right next to them appear names more respectable in matters of religion, like Du Perron, Scaliger, Montaigne, Descartes, Malebranche and even Garasse!

Reimann declares that our author has achieved great renown because of the violent opposition made to the *Sagesse*. He has read the work himself and he has found in it some good and some bad. This historian knows how not to compromise himself by taking sides.

In the latter part of the century, a French historian, Savérien,[59] in his *Histoire des Philosophes Modernes*, places Charron among the best moralists of the period around 1600. He believes that the *Sagesse* has satisfied a need felt since antiquity and never filled. It gives us a complete theory of wisdom gathered from ancient and contemporary literature and presents it in the way that the *sage* should understand and practise it. Savérien gives an excellent abstract of the *Sagesse* and his comments are approving.

A few years later another abstract, or more exactly, a digest, of the *Sagesse* was published, and as it is not well known,[60] it seems appropriate to discuss it briefly. It is the *Analyse Raisonnée de la Sagesse de Charron*, published anonymously in London in 1789. According to Barbier's *Dictionnaire des ouvrages anonymes*[61] this is the work of J. P. L. de la Roche du Maine, Marquis de Luchet.[62] The Marquis de Luchet calls his work *Analyse*, but it would be more suitable to call it a digest as it is really a shortened version

---

[57] *Ibid.*, p. 512.

[58] Jacob F. Reimanni, *Historia universalis athèismi et atheorum falso et merito suspectorum apud Judaeos, ethnicos, Christianos, mahu metanos ordine chronologico descripta, ab suis initiis usque ad nostra tempora deducta*, Hildesiae: 1725.

[59] Savérien, *Histoire des philosophes modernes*, Paris: 1761.

[60] Sabrié is the only critic to mention it: *op. cit.*, p. 537.

[61] A. A. Barbier, *Dictionnaire des ouvrages anonymes*, Paris: Fechoz & Letouzey, 1882.

[62] J. P. L. de la Roche du Maine, Marquis de Luchet, *Analyse Raisonnée de la Sagesse de Charron*, 2 vols., London: 1789. Barbier mentions also a first edition in Amsterdam in 1763.

of the *Sagesse* and not an abstract with commentaries. He tells us himself in the foreword[63] that he does not want to make a kind of translation of the *Sagesse* but merely to use the simple language of Charron and rid the text of its tedious passages. He is presenting the reader with the heart of Charron's work and not his own interpretation of Charron's *Sagesse*. He seems to have understood fairly well our canon's intentions and warns the reader to interpret the *Sagesse* in a very vague and general way, keeping in mind that it is intended as a guide to behaving well in the path one has chosen, whatever one's station in life may be.

Luchet places Charron above the philosophers of antiquity[64] who are not too commendable because of their mores or of their disrespect for the gods. He feels humiliated as a man when he reads other works on morals because of their tendency to give a dark and unfavorable picture of humanity. But he denies having any admiration for Charron as a writer and philosopher, accusing him of tiring the reader with his style and repetitiousness, although one can't expect a theologian to write like a gentleman.[65] Whenever Luchet does not agree with Pierre Charron he says so in a footnote. Because of the interpretation he imposes on the *Sagesse*, he leaves out many chapters, not judging them necessary for a full understanding of the work.

Reminding us that Charron writes for scholars and preaches to the people,[66] he believes that Charron's profession of faith in God and in his Church should be kept in mind when reading his development of a *sagesse humaine* in which he has been careful not to introduce anything divine. If the tone is too bold in matters of politics, Luchet has toned it down in order to avoid official censure; he has also modernized the style whenever it is a help to understanding the work.[67]

Luchet mentions also that he published his *Analyse* only because Jean Jacques Rousseau (who had much esteem for Charron) had renounced his project of publishing a new edition of the *Sagesse*.[68] It was generally known that Rousseau was much interested in the *Sagesse*, but this is the first time that we learn that the

[63] Luchet, *op. cit.*, p. xxi.
[64] *Ibid.*, pp. xxvi-xxviii.
[65] *Ibid.*, p. xxxiv.
[66] *Ibid.*, p. xxxvi.
[67] *Ibid.*, p. xiv.
[68] *Ibid.*, p. xxii.

philosopher of Geneva had considered publishing an edition of it. There exists a 1618 edition of the *Sagesse* which had been given to Rousseau by the Marquise de Créqui.[69] But when Rousseau quotes Charron (and he did so only once, in the *Emile*),[70] he quotes from the 1601 first edition of the *Sagesse*, and not from his own. This would seem to indicate that he was interested enough in Charron to have consulted more than one edition of his works. As a matter of fact, Sabrié thinks that some of the main ideas not only of the *Emile* but also of the *Discours sur les Sciences et les Arts* and the *Discours sur l'Origine de l'Inégalité parmi les Hommes* could be found condensed in various paragraphs of the *Sagesse*.[71] We will consider this idea in greater detail later when we study the works of Charron.

In the nineteenth and twentieth centuries, as literary criticism took new directions, the criticism of Charron changed radically. The *Sagesse* was no longer studied in order to furnish ammunition to one side or the other, but for its own merits; and for the past one hundred and thirty years this criticism, often similarly formulated but almost always unchanged, has given the portrait of Charron that we now have, that of a priest-philosopher, following closely in his writings the thought of his master, Montaigne.

Sainte-Beuve makes his first casual mention of Charron in his *Causerie* on Montaigne:[72] "Charron son disciple le suit pas à pas." Then later he devoted two *causeries* to Charron.[73] This was in December, 1854. Sainte-Beuve tells us that much had been said and written lately about Montaigne, his friend La Boétie, his "fille d'alliance" Mademoiselle de Gournay, and that it was time for something to be said about his disciple Charron, who was read so much in the 1600's and who is so forgotten today. He wants to define his character, his merit, and his exact relationship with Montaigne since he seems quite shocked to have found that some "beaux esprits, médiocres juges en cela",[74] had found Charron equal or superior to Montaigne. This is an important point to remember

[69] This volume of *De la Sagesse* is at the Bibliothéque Nationale and bears Rousseau's signature with the mention: given by Mme. la Marquise de Créqui, Sabrié, *op. cit.*, p. 529.

[70] J. J. Rousseau, *Oeuvres Complètes*, 8 vols., Paris: 1858, Vol. II, p. 88.

[71] Sabrié, *op. cit.*, pp. 529 f.

[72] C. A. Sainte-Beuve, *Causeries du Lundi*, Paris: Garnier Frères, 1868, Vol. IV, p. 77.

[73] *Ibid.*, pp. 236-270.

[74] *Ibid.*, p. 236.

because Sainte-Beuve repeats it frequently throughout his two articles. He concludes with the judgment of Jean de Muller on Montaigne,[75] who read the *Essays* for the sake of his health, "comme on prend un calmant", because Montaigne is "si serein, si spirituel, si content". And Sainte-Beuve says in conclusion that the continuing satisfaction which is renewed from generation to generation by the reading of immortal geniuses will never be obtained by reading Charron. Sainte-Beuve's study of Charron was the most complete one up to that time and it includes the comparison of some passages of the *Essays* with some of the *Sagesse*. Delboulle was to continue this line of thought in his article *Charron Plagiaire de Montaigne.*[76] The author of the Lundis had warned us in the beginning of his articles: "Le jugement que j'aurai à donner ne sera pas nouveau." After reviewing both sides of the criticism on Charron, Sainte-Beuve clears him of the charges of impiety and thinks of him as a helpful guide, useful in his time, who gave in his *Sagesse* a didactical reworking of the *Essays*, and henceforth deserves praise and a place in the history of literature in the shadow of his master Montaigne.[77]

Subsequently, as we are going to see, several major studies on Montaigne and on the evolution of the French thought from Montaigne to Pascal have devoted a chapter or a series of chapters to Charron, and histories of French literature have given him some attention, but since the time of Sainte-Beuve the general pattern of the criticism of Charron has not changed greatly; a few details have been added, a few clarifications made and some additional material brought to light, but Charron is still thought of as "the disciple of Montaigne".

Paul Bonnefon, librarian of the Arsenal Library, devoted one hundred pages to Charron in his *Montaigne et ses amis.*[78] He reviewed very carefully all the known facts, correcting some inaccuracies of his predecessors[79] and discovering some new facts like the argument of the *Pari de Pascal* in the *Trois Vérités.*[80]

---

[75] *Ibid.*, p. 270.

[76] Delboulle, *Charron Plagiaire de Montaigne*, *RHL*, Vol. 7, Paris: 1900, p. 284.

[77] Sainte-Beuve, *Causeries*, p. 269.

[78] Paul Bonnefon, *Montaigne et ses amis*, 2 vols., Paris: Armand Colin, 1898, Vol. II, pp. 213-311.

[79] *Ibid.*, p. 216, for instance: Pierre Charron received his Doctorats in laws from Montpellier and not from Bourges or Orléans.

[80] *Ibid.*, p. 255.

In the conclusion of his *Causerie* on Charron, Sainte-Beuve declared our canon to be "un problème psychologique et biographique non encore résolu",[81] and Bonnefon succeeded in his endeavor to throw some light on this problem. He is also the first to make use of the *Lettres inédites de Charron à La Rochemaillet*, published after Sainte-Beuve's work had been done, by Lucien Auvray.[82]

A few years later, in 1909, Fortunat Strowski in the first part of his *Histoire du Sentiment Religieux en France au XVII*ᵉ *Siècle*,[83] went a little further than Bonnefon in answering Sainte-Beuve's question about Charron. He is interested in Charron chiefly because the *Sagesse* helped to mold the mind of the *libertin* in the seventeenth century. He considers Pierre Charron's *Sagesse* as "le livre capital, le bréviaire des incrédules",[84] and hence leans very much on Garasse for the interpretation of our canon's philosophy, although he disapproves of moral charges made by the latter. It is interesting to note, however, that Strowski recognizes that between 1615 and 1635 the *Sagesse* had in France the importance that the *Essays* were to have later.[85] But it is a mosaic, says he, and "Charron y pille à pleines mains, y copie à pages entières Montaigne et Du Vair", and he cites Garasse as a proof:

> *La Sagesse* et *la Vérité* ne sont que des pensées sombres et plates, ou des traductions mal entendues, ou des larrecins mal déguisés de Michel de Montaigne, qui fut plus homme de bien que son plagiaire. Il n'y a pas une citation latine dans *la Sagesse* et *la Vérité* qui ne soit mot pour mot dans les *Essais* de Montaigne.[86]

We will show later that this type of judgment on Charron has been constantly repeated without any basis of proof.[87]

---

[81] Sainte-Beuve, *Causeries*, p. 269.

[82] Louis Auvray, *Lettres de Pierre Charron*, *RHL*, Paris: Colin, 1894, p. 231.

[83] Fortunat Strowski, *Histoire du Sentiment Religieux en France au XVII*ᵉ *Siècle, Pascal et son Temps, 1*ᵉʳ *Partie, de Montaigne à Pascal*, Paris: Plon, 1909, pp. 159-211.

[84] *Ibid.*, p. 161.

[85] *Ibid.*, p. 165.

[86] *Ibid.*, p. 176.

[87] Infra, p. 128.

Strowski defines the *Sagesse* as the effort of a priest who attempts to use the principles of stoicism to purify and cleanse the soul in which faith resides, fearing that the corruption of the container would corrupt the content. Stoicism will degenerate into scepticism but, according to our critic, if Montaigne's doubt was inspired by human kindness, Charron's doubt is due to pure intellectual pride. He has only contempt for the average man, he is completely undemocratic, he uses scepticism to raise himself above his fellowmen.[88]

Strowski ends his criticism of Charron by analysing in detail the parts of the *Sagesse* which so delighted the *libertins* of the first half of the seventeenth century. It shows how the free thinker becomes a deist as Charron teaches him to make a distinction between God and religion. This was not Charron's intention, however, Strowski adds, as he thought religion itself was well defended by the *Trois Vérités,* and he would have been the most astonished of men to discover that his *Sagesse* was being used in an attempt to defeat its actual purpose.[89]

Among the histories of French literature which mention Charron, we include those of Faguet and Brunetière. Emile Faguet[90] introduces our canon as the main disciple of Montaigne. He is not too exact in the details, telling us for instance, that Charron had been a Carthusian or that he wrote the *Discours Chrétiens contre la Ligue.*[91] Then quoting Sainte-Beuve in calling the *Sagesse* an "édition didactique des *Essais*", he concludes by saying that he does not perceive a preacher under the writer but an orator under a preacher writing a book.

Ferdinand Brunetière[92] has a short but rather complete section on Charron, and for the first time we hear a dissonance: "Charron)... à aucun degré n'est, comme on le prétent, le continuateur de Montaigne et l'heritier de son scepticisme." Brunetière notes

[88] Strowski, *op. cit.,* p. 181.

[89] *Ibid.,* p. 165.

[90] Emile Faguet, *Histoire de la Littérature Française,* Paris: Plon, 1901, Vol., I, p. 301.

[91] The *Discours Chrétiens* were editions of Charron's sermons. Faguet meant probably one of the two *Discours* posthumously published by the care of La Rochemaillet in 1606. It should be: *Discours chrestien qu'il n'est permis ny loisible à un subject, pour quelque cause et raison que ce soit, de se liguer, bandèr et rebeller contre son Roy,* Paris: Luclerc, 1606.

[92] Ferdinand Brunetière, *Histoire de la Littérature Française Classique,* Vol. II, Le XVIIe Siècle, Paris: Delagrave, 1912, pp. 73-76.

that although he imitates Montaigne, he is at the antipode of Montaigne's point of view, since he never renounced his right to think and judge with his reason. Along with Henri Busson, he considers Charron the founder of an original code of morality in France.

In two different works[93] Busson has studied the evolution of religious thought and of rationalism in France, and has given Charron the important place he deserves. In the same literary vein the most important of all works, as far as our interest lies, is Sabrié's *De l'Humanisme au Rationalisme*[94] which as we already know is devoted entirely to Pierre Charron, his work and his influence. Everything which by 1912 was known about our canon finds its proper place in Sabrié's book.

The general interpretation has not changed from the one given by Sainte-Beuve, just the details. Sainte-Beuve's views are still held by Sabrié as Faguet and Lanson[95] had held them. In his *Avant-propos* he tells us that "Instructive par sa diversité, l'oeuvre de Charron est curieuse par l'intime contradiction qu'elle renferme". Sainte-Beuve had left this question pending, and Bonnefon and Strowski had tried to help solve it. Sabrié continues:

> Charron a été l'ami et le disciple de Montaigne... c'est l'herbier de Montaigne. La pensée de Montaigne ne perd que ses charmes littéraires à être étudiée dans la *Sagesse*..., Charron nous expliquera Montaigne, après l'avoir imité, précisément par l'imitation qu'il en a faite.[96]

Thus, the evaluation of Charron's significance is still that of Sainte-Beuve: "Let us study Charron to understand Montaigne better. The disciple will help throw some light on the master."

Sabrié divided his study into three parts, studying the man, his works, and his influence. Among the new contributions found in this very complete and revealing work, we should mention an exhaustive examination of the *Archives de la Gironde*; this study furnished some new material and further illuminated other material

[93] Henri Busson, *La Pensée religieuse française de Charron à Pascal*, Paris: J. Vrin, 1933; *Les sources et le développement du rationalisme dans la littérature française de la renaissance*, Paris: Letouzey et Ané, 1922.

[94] Sabrié, *op. cit.*

[95] Gustave Lanson, "Pierre Charron", *Grande Encyclopédie.*

[96] Sabrié, *op. cit.*, p. 4.

already known. Sabrié also pointed out one of the important sources of Charron not known until then: *L'Examen des aptitudes pour les sciences de Huarte.*[97] Savinien d'Alquié's translation cited by Sabrié was published in 1672 but Villey mentions an earlier translation by Gabriel Chappuis published in 1580.[98]

Juan Huarte,[99] a Spanish physician, is said to have been the precursor of the school of thought in the medical world which at the end of the last century sought to achieve an evaluation of the moral and intellectual aptitudes of man through a study of the intimate relationship between physical and intellectual characteristics. Among the different aptitudes which each individual may show only one can be developed to a maximum, and corresponding to this aptitude there is only one field in which an individual may excel. It follows that it is important to recognize the factors regulating the development of these aptitudes. They are warmth and coldness, humidity and dryness. According to Huarte therefore, man's IQ (the variable) is a function of these four paremeters. Their action is both internal (their part in the composition of the body) or external (the climate).

Since Sabrié's work, interest in Charron has been limited to his place in the evolution of rationalism in France. We have already mentioned Busson's work several times. Following the same general train of thought the Abbé Bremond and René Pintard have furnished us with very detailed studies[100] of *libertin* and religious thought in France. Although the Abbé Brémond refers only in passing to Pierre Charron in his study of prayer,[101] Pintard[102] keeps Charron in his usual place after his master Montaigne and, obviously ignoring Charron's stand on that matter,[103] accuses him of willingly neglecting faith in separating his *Sagesse* from faith. A few pages

---

[97] *Ibid.*, p. 255.

[98] Pierre Villey, *Les Sources et l'Evolution des Essais de Montaigne*, 2 vols., Paris: Hachette, 1908, Vol. II, p. 366; Chappuis' translation was called: *L'Examen des Esprits.*

[99] Juan Huarte, *Examen de Ingenios para las Ciéncias*, Barcelona: Biblioteca Clásica Española, 1884.

[100] H. Brémond, *Histoire littéraire du sentiment religieux en France depuis la fin des guerres de religion jusqu'à nos jours*, 11 vols., Paris: Blond et Gay, 1916-1936; René Pintard, *Le libertinage érudit dans la première moitié du XVIIeme Siècle*, Paris: Boivin, 1943.

[101] Brémond, *op. cit.*, Vol. 7, Ch. I.

[102] Pintard, *op. cit.*, p. 61.

[103] Supra, p. 18.

later,[104] taking into account the *Discours Chrestiens* published after the *Sagesse* in 1604 (but written certainly before the *Sagesse*),[105] Pintard sees in Charron an evolution ranging from absolute "fideism"[106] to relative "fideism". For the rest Pintard bases his approach on the work of Sabrié which he says was so finely and picturesquely completed by the Abbé Brémond. This might be either a mild appreciation or a mild criticism of an article of the Abbé Brémond entitled "La Folle 'Sagesse' de Pierre Charron".[107] Pintard must be referring to this article, since other mention of Pierre Charron in the Abbé's opus are only in passing, as we have already stated.

In this article, which was published shortly after the publication of Sabrié's dissertation on Pierre Charron, the Abbé Brémond violently attacked Sabrié in a manner not too different from the one so dear to Father Garasse. Calling Sabrié's auxiliary thesis, *Les Idées Religieuses de Balzac,* a thin piece of research, he seems amazed that Sabrié's opus on Pierre Charron could have been passed by his watchful committee at his final examinations. Accusing Sabrié of having followed the University tradition in exposing Garasse's criticism on Charron and making of the Jesuit nothing "qu'un bouffon ou qu'un forcené",[108] he presents to us a picture, a la Garasse, of a Charron, shadow of Montaigne, almost smelling of the fire which punishes heretics; and he concludes by telling us that a third grade preacher (this is not much of an appreciation of a preacher who by the tone of his sermons contributed to the evolution of the art of preaching in sixteenth-century France), Charron is not much of a humanist, a miserable one, very inferior to that other humanist, François Garasse.

In recent times we find Pierre Charron studied in relation to the study of stoicism in France in the first half of the seventeenth century. The opinion of the author, Father Julien Eymard, on Charron[109] is still in line with Sainte-Beuve's: "Après Montaigne, plus

---

[104] Pintard, *op. cit.,* p. 67.

[105] Infra, p. 95.

[106] A system which places in faith the knowledge of basic truths.

[107] Henri Brémond, "La Folle 'Sagesse' de Pierre Charron", *Correspondant,* July, 1913, Vol. 252, p. 357.

[108] *Ibid.,* p. 360.

[109] Julien Eymard, O. F. M. Cap.: "Le Stoicisme en France dans la 1er moitié du XVIIe Siècle, Pierre Charron, Le Stoicisme Chrétien, Guillaume du Vair", *Etudes Franciscaines,* Vol. II, Paris: December, 1951.

ou moins héritier de sa pensée, pillant ici, pillant là, Pierre Charron composait son livre."[110]

In summary, it can be said that the fundamental attitude toward Charron and his role in French literature has not changed since Charles Sorel gave the first objective and unbiased criticism on our canon in his *Bibliothèque Françoise*[111] of 1664. Subsequent critics have simply elaborated and developed the ideas of Sorel on the subject. They have leaned however more towards the adverse criticism inspired by the followers of Garasse and Mersenne. After a brief review of the background of the period and the life and works of the author we will endeavor to present a new picture of the canon of Condom. This chapter has shown that the succession of critics have never proved the traditional assumption that Charron was a disciple of Montaigne. We will see that Charron was an independent and original thinker and that his connection with Montaigne was only that they both lived in the same era and were under the same general influence.[112]

---

[110] *Ibid.*, p. 389.

[111] Supra, pp. 32-33.

[112] Professor Rice's *The Renaissance Idea of Wisdom* [Eugene F. Rice, Jr., *The Renaissance Idea of Wisdom* (Harvard Historical Monographs, XXXVII). Cambridge, Mass.: Harvard University Press, 1958] was received after this book had gone to press. Rice examines the evolution of Wisdom from the Middle Ages to the end of the Renaissance and after studying Charron in detail reaches the conclusion that Charron's "Sagesse" best represents the Renaissance ideal of Wisdom (p. 215). Here again, although Charron is given a much more important role than usual, the traditional view of the disciple of Montaigne, founder of a secularized code of morality has been preserved.

CHAPTER III

CHARRON AND HIS AGE

The age in which Charron lived is one of the saddest in the history of France. The era of optimism and faith in the future which had marked the times of Francis the First had changed into a spirit of depression and disillusionment. The religious struggles of the latter half of the sixteenth century brought in their wake suffering and distrust, and men were seeking for new values around which to organize their basis for living.

We want to review the general lines of the political and religious struggle, bringing in some details too often neglected, such as the history of the reception (or rather non-reception) of the decrees of the Council of Trent by the King, the Etats Généraux and the Gallican Church. This will explain in part the evolution of the ideas of Charron as an individual and not as a member of the school of thought of Montaigne in which he has been placed by biographers until now. He was, because of his position, intimately involved in the mighty political and religious struggle which the Council wanted to regulate by reforms and in which the high nobility, the King, and the Church had so much at stake.

Francis the First was determined to see the Renaissance succeed in France. The conservatives, led by the Sorbonne, did their best to hold on to the past, but the King, backed by men like Budé and the Du Bellays, and helped by the *Concordat* with the Pope, continued to further the coming of the new age in his kingdom. New enlightened bishops were nominated, the *lecteurs royaux* were created, and the Sorbonne saw a *Parlement* of younger men, educated in the new age of enlightenment, refuse her the censure of the *lecteurs royaux* in 1534, and even in 1536 there took place the reform of the "Sacerrima Facultas": the Faculty of Theology.

The *Tiersparti,* a conciliation party, was formed and Francis, with the agreement of a Medici Pope who had just given his niece in marriage to the French crown prince, was working for a reconciliation between the Holy See and his allies, the German princes. However, the French refugees in Germany, under the leadership of Farel, were opposed to any reconciliation and probably had a hand in the *affaire des placards,*[1] as a means of breaking the negotiations.

The reactionary elements in France had been awaiting an opportunity of this kind. They lost no time in persuading Francis that here was positive proof that the Protestants aimed at nothing less than the destruction of the kingdom. There ensued a kind of mass hysteria. Arrests and executions brought on retaliation in the form of desecration of Catholic services and even the murder of priests while they were performing their duties. And then, in counter-retaliation, the murderers were lynched. An amnesty declared in 1536 brought little relief. Negotiations with the German princes were broken off and the reform movement made such progress that Francis was faced with a real internal problem. During the ten years following the Holy Alliance of the Catholic princes (1537-1547), repression of the Protestants continued.

Pierre Charron was born in the midst of these terrible years, in 1541. When he was four years old the massacre of the Vaudois took place, almost against the will of a Francis weakened by disease. Francis died in 1547 and his son Henri II, weak in character, was under the influence of the leading spirit of the Holy Alliance and the partisan of repression: Anne de Montmorency.

Things had by then reached a point where religion had become a political football; the powerful noble families were aware of the fact that whichever party controlled the King would emerge the victor in the religious struggle. The Guises of Lorraine, with their cardinals succeeding Montmorency in the King's council, identified themselves with the party of reaction and at the same time the fiery new King of Navarre, Antoine de Bourbon, chose to assert himself by aligning his followers with the reformers. Henceforth the King of Navarre became the nominal leader of the Protestants.

---

[1] During the night of the seventeenth to the eighteenth of October 1534, posters were placed all over Paris and the largest cities and even on the King's door. The title shows the kind of popular feeling they were meant to arouse: "Articles Véritables sur les horribles, grands et insupportables abus de la messe papale inventée contre la Sainte Cène".

Thus the Reform was transformed from a sporadic explosion of protest into an opposition political party.

Montluc had said that if you could have gathered together in one council room the Queen, Monsieur de Guise, the Prince of Condé, and the Admiral of Coligny you could have made them confess that it was much more than religion which had impelled three hundred thousand men to kill each other.[2] As early as 1561 Joyeuse suggested that the insurrections in the South were aimed at something other than religion, and the Venetian Ambassador Michiel and the papal nuncio agreed in 1575 that religion was playing only a secondary role in the civil war and that "Il male veramente non e di religione ma di regno".[3] Furthermore, as always in times of duress, people started to question the legitimacy of ancient institutions. For many the word *Ligue*, even if it was a *Sainte Ligue*, meant much more than a union for the same holy cause, and was also a main threat to the royal power. Queen Catherine saw the danger clearly and in a letter of December 25, 1575 cautioned her son about it.[4]

Here is what was stated by the Manifesto of the Holy League, which was spread all over France by the Duke de Guise:

> In the name of the Holy Trinity, this association of Princes and gentlemen plan to re-establish the law of God in its entity and to re-establish and retain His Holy Service acording to the manner of the Holy, Catholic, Apostolic, and Roman Church; to keep King Henry III in the state and authority due to him but without prejudice to what will be ordered by the *Etats Généraux*. But they plan furthermore to restore to the provinces (could it be to the dukes and counts, heads of these provinces) the old rights, pre-eminence, franchises and liberties that they enjoyed under the Christian King Clovis, and forewarn that they will be even more enjoyable and profitable when found again under the Holy League's leadership.[5]

---

[2] Gabriel Hanotaux, *Histoire de la nation française*, Vol. IV, *Histoire Politique de 1515 à 1804*, by Louis Madelin, Paris: Plon, 1924, p. 97.

[3] *Ibid.*, p. 98.

[4] Hector De la Ferrière, *Lettrès de Catherine de Medici*, Paris: Imprimerie Nationale, 1895, p. 181.

[5] Ernest Lavisse, *Histoire de France*, Vol. VI, *La Réforme et la Ligue*, by Jean H. Mariéjol, Paris: Hachette, 1911, p. 175.

Cities and townships were graciously invited to join the League freely but were secretly warned that if they didn't they would be considered enemies. And King Henry III, in dire need of money, gave permission to join to all that paid 8,000 pounds to his treasury.

The wars of religion began in 1562. These were not revolts and repressions but civil wars between organized parties striving for political gains in the name of religion. Charles IX succeeded Henry II, and Henry III succeeded Charles IX. Catherine de Medici was regent during the minority of Charles IX, and later continued to have at times an all-powerful voice and at other times a very feeble influence in the affairs of the kingdom. For almost thirty years civil wars tore France apart, interrupted by short truces marked by occasional changes of direction in the royal policy.

One of these changes was to cause the massacre of St. Bartholomew. Charles IX was finally growing up and had become enthusiastic about the project of the Admiral de Coligny to divert the energy spent in the civil strife towards national gain on the northeastern borders at the expense of the Spanish Low Countries. Catherine de Medici was not necessarily against such a project, but she was privately of the opinion that once France was at war with Spain, France and her governing body would be in the hands of the Admiral. The Guises and Catherine, who had personally supported Coligny before, resented the influence of the Huguenots on the King. Henri de Guise, well informed of all that was happening around the King, made use of some undersecretaries serving the crown to inform Catherine that it was most urgent that she intervene with her son, as the Admiral and the Huguenot party were usurping her influence on him. For a few days the Admiral and the Queen Mother fought for Charles' affection. Feeling that the King's enthusiasm for the war in the Low Countries was cooling, Coligny told Catherine: "The King is renouncing the war with Spain; God wishes him not to be waging another war (a civil war) over which he would have no control."[6] The Queen understood this as a bold threat and resolved then that Coligny should die.

Into this decision entered no religious fanaticism, and the only other possible inspiration, beside the fear the Queen Mother had of the Admiral, was the lesson in politics taught her by Machiavelli's *The Prince*.

---

[6] Hanotaux, *op. cit.*, p. 116.

On the twenty-second of August a paid assassin missed his target and succeeded only in wounding the Admiral in the arm. The King, unaware of the chess game being played around his person, swore that he would punish the guilty man. One of the Guises, the Duke d'Aumale, persuaded Catherine that if she didn't act quickly to change her son's mind her life would be in as great danger as theirs. Catherine then confessed the truth to Charles and pleaded with him to order the assassination of Coligny and of the Huguenot chiefs then gathered in Paris for the marriage of Henri de Navarre to Marguerite. "If he didn't" she added, "no one would ever believe that she and the Guises had acted without his knowledge when ordering the attempt on the Admiral's life."[7]

The young King felt he was caught between his oath to punish those who had ordered the assassination and delivering his mother to the judges. History says that in an excess of rage Charles is supposed to have said: "Since you believe it is right for the Admiral to be disposed of, then I want it so, but exterminate also all of the Huguenots, so that no one will live to reproach me for my decision."[8] Thus began the ill-fated day of the twenty-fourth of August, 1572, the feast of Saint Bartholomew. Mass hysteria did the rest.

Pierre Charron was then just over thirty years old. At this time he probably lived in Bordeaux. He had just completed his doctorate in canon and civil law in March 1571 at Montpellier. During his six-year stay there he even had been very much in the midst of these terrible political and religious strifes. As we will see later, he was prisoner of the Protestants from November 19, 1567 to June 8, 1568. Truly French law schools were good schools of moderation. The young graduates would usually register with the Parlements, and we know how wise and relatively moderate the Parlements of Paris and of the provinces were during the religious wars. Pierre Charron must have acquired this tolerance, since his tone in the *Trois Vérités* and in the *Sagesse* show evidence of it, and he never showed bitterness for what had happened to him in Montpellier, or for that matter even mentioned it.

After the Saint Bartholomew massacre, excesses were not uncommon in both camps. A short truce would come from time to time to allow reorganisation. When, after the death of Charles IX,

---

[7] *Ibid.*, p. 118.
[8] *Ibid.*, p. 118.

Henri III came back from Poland to become King, he found himself obliged to take orders and not to reign. He tried to head the League in order not to have to fight it, but the Guises were becoming more and more arrogant, and we find the weak French king almost powerless between two great parties: Henri de Navarre had become the leader and the protector of the Protestants.

When Henri III asked money from the Parlements, they appointed a watch-dog committee to see how it was spent. Already a favorite saying was going around: "Pas d'argent, pas de Suisses", and without a Swiss guard the King was even more powerless.

The convocation of the *Etats Généraux* at Blois did not improve the situation greatly, and it is thus that Henri, deprived of his capital and of most of his domains, saw in the assassination of the Guises his only path to power. The League's control of the *Etats Généraux* exasperated the King, and when to this insubordination was added the invasion of the march of Salluces by the Duke of Savoy with no attempt on the part of the French people to face the invaders, Henri III felt that the country was being betrayed. The *Etats* of Blois at the same time proclaimed that their decisions would henceforth have power of law, and the King then resolved to strike a blow at the head of the League by having the Duke and the Cardinal de Guise assassinated. "A présent, je suis roi", he wrote to the papal nuncio after the Guises' death.

But this double murder did to the League what the murder of St. Bartholomew had done to the Huguenots. Henri III was lost and powerless against the League. Henri de Navarre saved him and was marching on Paris in his company to recapture the capital. It was of no avail. The Parisian militia had been beaten at Senlis, but the Parisian preachers of the League were demanding a Brutus to rid the kingdom of France of her unworthy monarch. On the first of August 1589, in Saint Cloud, a fanatic Dominican monk, Clément, inflicted a deadly wound on the last of the Valois Kings. Henri III died the next day, naming Henri de Navarre as his heir and begging him to embrace the Catholic faith.

One last series of events was still to sadden France before she achieved the peace she had been longing for. King Philip of Spain wanted the throne for his daughter the Infanta, and because of personal ambition some of the nobility were ready to help. The last of the Guise brothers, Mayenne, hoped to be elected to the throne, but he had to back the demands of Spain. Philip did not wait for a decision of the *Etats Généraux*; instead he entered Gascony and sent troops into northern France and even to Paris. The

Duke of Savoy was enlarging his possessions at the expense of south-eastern France.

The country was falling into shreds and a preponderant majority of Frenchmen was becoming desirous of an end to internal strife in order to save themselves from the invaders. Their hope was to crystallise in spite of all opposition around the person of the legitimate heir, Henri de Navarre, Henry IV of France. His conversion on the twenty-fifth of July, 1593 in the old basilica of Saint Denis was the awaited catalyst, and within a year most of the old Leaguers and the rebel cities followed the new King with enthusiasm. Peace was finally coming to the kingdom of France, but deep changes and reforms in the moral and philosophic make-up of the country had taken place through these years of suffering and duress.

The Protestant movement had brought to light the abuses and the necessity for reforms in the Catholic Church. The Council of Trent, which convened on May 22, 1542, and which was to last for twenty years, marks the beginning of the counter-reform movement.

The propagators of Lutheranism and Calvinism in France had gained much ground, especially the latter. They justified the necessity for their attitude by the conditions which were threatening to destroy the spirit of holiness in the Church. In monasteries, upon episcopal seats, and up to the Holy See itself, the spirit of worldliness, avarice, ambition and frivolous and sensual pleasure had often prevailed.

The responsibilities weighing on the shoulders of the Council were therefore enormous. They had not only to correct the damage done to dogma by the reform movement, but also to reform the clergy and correct the abuses which were then prevalent.

The Council was also under pressure from the jealous monarchs. Charles V wanted reforms enabling him to deal with the German princes, while Francis I wanted to manage them as if they were his allies. Later Catherine de Medici pressed for more concessions to insure the good will and perhaps the adhesion of the Protestants.

Henri II and Charles IX wanted not only action against the Huguenots who were endangering their power, but also the end of benefice-holding *in absentia* by Roman prelates. The Holy See was much concerned with the habit of the French Kings of considering monasteries, bishoprics and vicarages political prizes with often little, if any, consideration for the interests of the Church. All this explains why the Council of Trent lasted so long. It was finally terminated on December 4, 1563.

Its decrees[9] set rules for the training, the life and the holding of offices and benefices by the clergy. The opening and maintenance of adequate seminaries were recommended. The celebration of the Eucharist, the administration of the Sacraments, the control of the preaching function, the justification and the value of good works and all the points under attack by the reformed churches were also covered by the decrees.

In a letter to Charles IX, Pius IV recommended that residence in benefices be enforced at all costs and that dispensation should be given only for reasons of state, such as ambassadorship or other political appointments made in the interest of the nation. A good example of grants of Church benefices as political bounty was the case of the Cardinal of Lorraine, although he could claim exemption from the Pope's order because he was ambassador at large and was at this time the head of the Gallican Church delegation to the Council. Nevertheless, residence in benefices would have been an insoluble problem for the Cardinal, since to his Dukedom and bishopric of Reims he added the Abbacies of the monasteries of Saint Denis, of Fécamp, of Marmontier, of Souillac, of Moutier, of Saint Martin, and of Saint Remy.[10]

For this reason the Cardinal of Lorraine would have been the first hurt by enforcement of rules of residence. Nevertheless, the Pope was aware that the Cardinal's support of his project was absolutely necessary, since if he submitted others could only follow suit. The Pope gained the Cardinal's help by letting him expect to become a kind of Cardinal Primate of France, the supreme arbiter of the Gallican Church, answering directly to Rome. Playing politics, Pius consulted Catherine and Charles IX on the possible elevation of Lorraine to this high position, being perfectly aware that they would be very much against it since this would add to the Guises' strong political position a complete dominance over the Church of France. However, if the promise were not fulfilled the responsibility would rest with the King of France.

By this time the French court had become annoyed with the evident intention of the Pope to accomplish a complete reform of the Church by the Council, a reform which would include curtailing the privileges of the princes and nobles (which would result in a

---

[9] Konrad Algermissen, *Christian Denominations,* Translated by Rev. Joseph W. Grundner, St. Louis: B. Herder Book Co., 1948, 3d ed., p. 529.

[10] Henri Martin, *Histoire de France,* Vo. II, Paris: Furne, 1857, p. 81.

great loss of regular income), but would do nothing towards furnishing the financial and political aid promised for the repression of the heresy in France.

Informed that the personal envoys of the sovereigns partaking in the Council would have to swear to observe the reforms ordered by the said Council at its conclusion, Charles IX ordered his two envoys to leave at the first favorable opportunity, which they did when the question of reforming the privileges of the princes was brought up. The Church of France therefore was represented at the conclusion of the Council, but not the King. And this is why the decrees of the Council were never ratified officially in France. Before the decrees of the Council of Trent could become legal measures in France, the King had to accept the Council's reforms and the Parlement to register them, and this was never done.

However, the French clergy was aware of the necessity for the reform and generally followed the Council's decrees and endeavored to have them accepted by the *Etats Généraux*. It was not until 1615 when the clerical delegation at the *Etats Généraux*, becoming finally aware of the conflict between secular and spiritual powers, issued a declaration promising to abide by the decrees of the Council of Trent. Actually, this was only a confirmation of an action taken at the convocation of the *Etats* in 1572 when the clergy had placed the question of recognition of the Council's decrees as the first article on their agenda. Furthermore the young King Louis XIII and the Regent Marie de Medicis were favorable to the declaration which kept them free from any personal controversy with the Holy See.

It is very important to keep in mind that the reform prescribed by the Council of Trent was deemed imperative by all parties concerned. The disagreement was on the timing of the publication and on the means of enforcing the decrees.

Some of the Popes, such as Pius IV, had made great demands without weighing the civil interests of the sovereigns. Or again the King was willing to abandon some of his privileges over the Church, but a too Gallican Parlement would not let him do so. It is to be noted that Henri IV had to accept the Council as a condition of his abjuration, but the Parlement refused to register the King's acceptance. The Parlement thought it was defending the King against himself.

Although the Council's decrees never became laws, they gained immediate obedience and respect. The numerous letters of the popes to the bishops and the great power in France of the Cardinal de Guise, one of the Council's principal collaborators, were to bring good results. The best deterrent to any infraction of the decrees was the knowledge that it would be immediately reported to Rome by the papal nuncio, or exploited as a political issue by the Huguenots. Bishops and their Chapters of Canons had not only to abide by the decrees but also to see that priests and clerics followed the new Catholic reform. Certainly one of the best answers to the Huguenot movement and to its criticism of the Catholics was for the Church to show good faith by observing the Council's reforms and to deserve henceforth to occupy the religious position it had held until then in the nation.

Pierre Charron occupied many canonships in the Southwest with the post of *théologal*.[11] In 1576 he was elected as *théologal* to the chapter of Bordeaux and shortly after elevated in addition by the Archbishop to the post of *écolâtre*. The appointment is significant; the thirty-five year old canon, just five years out of school, with a *doctorat* in *utroque jure*[12] that gave him *competence* in canon and civil laws, was responsible more than anyone else for the observance of the Council's decrees in his diocese. When he graduated, the Council's decrees were eight years old and must have been one of the most important recent additions to the law school curriculum.

Pierre Charron's role in the counter-reformation was again enhanced by his appointment in 1582, as a delegate from the Chapter of Bordeaux, to the provincial Council called in this city to fight the progress of heresy[13] and watch over the maintenance of ecclesiastic discipline. As we have seen before, these years were the crucial years when the French clergy had pledged itself to the Catholic reform without the help and backing of the civil power. Bordeaux was a most important see and Pierre Charron's position was certainly a sensitive and delicate one for a relatively young man lacking a great family name and political backing. Character, personal ability and worthiness were his qualifications, and this is a phase of Pierre Charron's career which has been neglected up to now.

As we reviewed the history of criticism on Pierre Charron, we saw that in their general picture of the development of rationalism in France critics were more worried about finding a niche for our

---

[11] The title of *théologal* gave a canon the right to teach theology and to preach in the cathedral, and the title of *écolâtre* gave the right to teach philosophy and humanities and the supervision of all the schools in the diocese.

[12] Infra, p. 60.

[13] Infra, p. 67.

canon in the shadow of Montaigne than about considering him as an important entity in an evolving intellectual society. It seems to me that to get a true picture of Charron it is important to keep in mind that while he was still alive and before he had become a figure in the history of philosophical thought, Pierre Charron, still a young canon, occupied very responsibile and sensitive Church positions in the region of Bordeaux. He secured these positions on merit alone, and because of his achievements in performing his duties he always received praise and constantly greater responsibilities until, near the end of his life, he decided to go into semiretirement in Condom to give more time to his studies and writings.

During the same period the Jesuits were being organized.[14] Ignatius of Loyola had, after twenty years of effort, obtained on September 27, 1540 by the papal bull *Regimini militantis ecclesiae*, the charter for his order, and he had been elected *General* of the order in April, 1541.

A strong order organized along military lines, the Jesuits had two definite purposes and duties: missionary work (principally in the Indies, but also in Germany and Austria), and education by preaching from the pulpit and teaching in colleges. Almost immediately they were given two colleges in Paris, the *Trésoriers*, and the *Lombards*.

The Church was then ready for the counter-reform. The Jesuits would be charged with the conquest of the upper classes through their colleges and their preaching. To the other orders, still popular with the masses, and to the secular clergy was left the task of carrying the reform to the lower classes.

These years were troubled years indeed. But if they were darkened by so much political and religious strife, they witnessed at the same time an overhauling of the physical body of the Catholic Church in France and the codification of a doctrine in the form of dogma. This had become necessary when the Renaissance had placed under scrutiny the teaching of the Church, measuring it against the norm of a culture derived from the ancients. It is also to be remembered that the popes and the French prelates who guided the Catholic reform were humanists. As we have mentioned before, Francis I had seen to it that the Renaissance and its culture triumphed in the universities and among the bishops and their schools.

---

[14] Henri Hauser, and Augustin Renaudet, *Les Débuts de l'Age Moderne, la Renaissance, et la Réforme*, Paris: 1929, p. 265.

Every one of Charron's protectors,[15] as we will see, was a distinguished scholar or a protector of men of letters. Condom, his last residence, was a center of culture. Du Bartas, the author of the *Semaines*, had been there a few years before. Gérard-Marie Imbert, poet and distinguished Hellenist, was a canon of that chapter, and the bishop Jean du Chemin was known as a poet and a humanist.

This is a brief glimpse at the period in which Pierre Charron was reared and educated. By the end of this period he had begun to make a name for himself. We will now place the life and the career of our canon against that background.

[15] Arnaus de Pontac, friend of letters, learned humanist, pious bishop of Bazas. Antoine d'Hébrard de Saint-Sulpice, bishop of Cahors, whose reputation as a great scholar was known even in Italy. Infra, pp. 64-81.

Chapter IV

CHARRON: THE MAN

We have very little factual information on Charron's life. All his biographers have complained about it and have drawn their information from the same source: *L'Eloge Véritable ou Sommaire Discours de la Vie de Pierre Charron Parisien Vivant Docteur ès Droicts* by G. M. D. R.[1] These initials stand for Gabriel Michel de la Rochemaillet, a lawyer from Angers, who was by far our canon's best and most devoted friend. He wrote the *Eloge* as a preface to the 1604 edition of Charron's *Sagesse.* After Charron's death, La Rochemaillet set himself the task of having the *De la Sagesse,* which had been impounded by the Sorbonne, released to the public. His diligence was rewarded when, through the intervention of President Jeannin, the objections of the Sorbonne and the rector of the University were overruled and the *De la Sagesse* was released for sale.

According to La Rochemaillet, and subsequently according to Charron's best biographers[2] (who were able to add a few details found in the Archives of Paris or of La Gironde), Pierre Charron was born in 1541 in the parish of Saint-Hilaire in Paris. He was one of the twenty-five children of Thibaud Charron (nine were by a former marriage).[3] His mother was Nicole de la Barre. In their

---

[1] Pierre Charron, *De la Sagesse,* Paris: David Douceur, 1607, *Eloge* by La Rochemaillet.

[2] Bonnefon, *op. cit.,* pp. 213-311; F. Strowski, *op. cit.,* pp. 166-211; Sabrié, *op. cit.,* pp. 19-141.

[3] Sabrié, *op. cit.,* p. 22, Sabrié must have checked the St. Hilaire Records. Other biographers had said four by a former marriage, but they limit the number of children to twenty-one. See Charron, *Sagessé,* 1607, *Eloge,* p. I.

biographies of Charron, other critics and biographers[4] state that none of his brothers survived him or had male descendents.

As previously noted, Pierre Charron was born, reared and educated in the years when the Renaissance was in full bloom in France. Rabelais' *Pantagruel* and *Gargantua* were only a decade old and the reading public was enraptured with this lyric source of love for nature and the ancients.

The young man of the Renaissance sought the bases of his education in a "Pantagruelic" fashion. He enjoyed many new sources of information which were now available: dictionaries, grammars, treatises on public speaking, critiques, histories and studies of versification.

According to La Rochemaillet, young Pierre studied at the University of Paris, and the history of his school training reminds one of a page of the *Pantagruel:*

> ...ils aurent soin de le faire instruire dés son jeune âge aux bonnes lettres: tellement que ayant appris en peu de temps les langues Grecques et Latine, dont y avait lors de célèbres professeurs en l'Université de Paris, il fit bonne provision des sciences libérales et humaines, et mesmes de la logique, éthique, physique et metaphysique: et depuis il estudia en droict civil et canon és Universitez d'Orléans et de Bourges, où il fut honoré du tiltre de degré de Docteur és droicts...[5]

La Rochemaillet, still our main source for Pierre Charron's biography, has proved untrustworthy in his account of his friend's education. Bonnefon found that after attending the Universities of Orléans and Bourges, Pierre Charron went to Montpellier where he secured his doctor's degree in canon and civil law and obtained his *lettres de licence* in *utroque jure* on the fifteenth of March 1571.[6] He was then thirty years old.

---

[4] A. Jal, *Dictionnaire Critique de Biographie et d'Histoire,* Paris: H. Plon, 1872; Sainte-Beuve, *Les Grands Ecrivains Français (études dès lundis),* Paris: Garnier Fréres, 1926, Vol. 3, pp. 252-259; Bayle, *op. cit.,* pp. 142-148.

[5] Charron, *Sagesse,* 1607, *Eloge,* pp. I f.

[6] Sabrié doublechecked the same information. Sabrié, *op. cit.,* p. 27, citing *Archives de la Girondè,* G. 798 F^{os} 441-442 showing that Pierre Charron had his diplomas registered in Bordeaux and that they were signed by Leonard Aguillonius vice chancellor of the University of Montpellier.

After this all of Charron's biographers tell us he then went to Paris and began the practice of law. But soon his "noble and courageous soul", again according to La Rochemaillet, refused to "court and caress and seek" the state attorneys and presidents of the court. He soon abandoned legal studies and the pursuit of law and entered the priesthood. From then on he devoted himself to the study of theology. However, this does not coincide with some new facts discovered by Mlle. Guiraud in the archives of the department of L'Héraut.[7]

In the "Régistre de matricules et baccalauréats de l'ancienne Université de Droit de Montpellier" Mlle Guiraud found that on July 26, 1565 the chapter of the cathedral had voted one hundred and fifty pounds a year for "Me Pierre Charron, séculier, qui preschera et lira". Therefore Pierre Charron was already a priest and had a law degree when he came to Montpellier at the age of twenty-four.

La Rochemaillet as the intimate friend of Pierre Charron should be trusted for the main facts in the life of Charron; only the chronology seems to be confused. He remembered the main events, but with the carelessness so common to his time he did not place them in the right order. As a matter of fact he scarcely gives any dates. It seems, however, that by her discovery Mlle Guiraud helps to bring together the data offered by La Rochemaillet and Bonnefon's findings. We could reconstruct this period of Charron's life something like this: after receiving a law degree from Bourges, Pierre Charron probably registered at the parlement of Paris and, soon becoming discouraged, decided to enter the priesthood. He began to preach and must have met success right away. This would explain why he was brought to Montpellier, where in spite of his tender years, he was given a teaching assignment and the responsibility of preaching the Advent. Within a year (September 15, 1566) the bishop, who was at the same time the titular head of the law school, and the chapter decided to attach Charron to themselves by making him *théologal* and canon. Two canons of the chapter called on bishop Guillaume Pellicier to express their appreciation for the new *théologal* he had given them. Mlle Guiraud also noticed on the register Charron's handwriting, a precise cursive so different from the local Gothic.

---

[7] L. Guiraud, "Le séjour de Pierre Charron à Montpellier, 1565-1569 et 1570-1571", *Bulletin Philologique et Historique*, Paris, 1913, pp. 107-117.

A year later Montpellier was besieged by the Protestants. The siege lasted forty-eight days. Twenty-eight churches and fourteen monasteries were destroyed and many others in the suburbs. The besieged were reduced to a diet of plain flour cake (neither salt nor honey was available) and finally had to eat horses, mules, and rats. Taken prisoner November 19, 1567, Charron was released when his ransom was paid on June 8, 1568 and went to take refuge in Maguelone. On November 22 he was back in Montpellier as vice-rector of the University and he received a degree of "Bachelier in utroque jure". A few months later he left Montpellier and was deleted from the payroll (May 2, 1569) "...attendu les notoires empeschementz qu'il ne peult prescher ny fere son estat dans ceste ville." Where did Charron go? Perhaps it was then that Charron joined the retinue of the Cardinal legate Georges d'Armagnac in Avignon. La Rochemaillet has given us this information, but no one has ever said when it happened. He was back in Montpellier in 1570 to preach for Advent the following Lent (1571) and the rest of the year.

He received his degrees of *Licencié* and *Docteur in utroque jure* the 15th and 19th of March 1571. It is therefore possible that Arnaus de Pontac heard him preach in the church of St. Paul in Paris in late 1571, and decided then to attach the youthful and talented preacher to his diocese of Bazas of which he was made bishop in 1571.[8]

It seems fairly certain that Charron came to Montpellier with a degree, and we know that he was already a priest. The entry on the register says "Me Pierre Charron, Seculier..." I think we can assume that once in Montpellier he was urged to continue his studies toward a *doctorat in utroque jure*. For a talented young man who should succeed in a church career a strong academic background would make up for the fact that he was not of high birth. His two sponsors when he was received *Bachelier* in Montpellier were the two eminent professors of civil law and canon law, Etienne Ranchin and Antoine Uzillis, and Charron was already the vice-rector of the University. Therefore, this conferring of a degree seems more likely to have been the validation of a previous degree from a less respected University (Orleáns or Bourges) than the old University of

---

[8] Sabrié does not think this was possible because he didn't known Charron was already a priest and a canon in Montpellier, and had been preaching for six or seven years.

Montpellier. This same procedure was also the rule at the old Spanish University of Salamanca.

If we accept this, then the brief experience of Charron at the bar mentioned by La Rochemaillet is still possible, and I repeat here that we should trust La Rochemaillet's word on that important turn in Charron's life. La Rochemaillet has proven himself to be our canon's most trusted and devoted friend. This possible experience at the Parlement of Paris and his law school background gave Charron his good training in oratory. Jean Bodin, Louis d'Orléans, Loisel, Michel de l'Hospital, all contemporaries of Charron, were among the best orators of France. Sabrié sees in that rhetorical training the germ of the oratorical reform which Charron was to carry to the pulpit.[9] This same training gave him a love for precise sentences and exact meanings. His sermons are a solid structure where clear and concise developments follow each new step in the argumentation and the final conclusion is a compact summary into which each one of these steps fits like a metallic cube into the implacable and clear-cut logic of the final proof. La Rochemaillet was right: the preacher was going to retain a *teincture du Palais.*

La Rochemaillet assures us that, although our canon never received his doctorate in theology, he was nevertheless worthy of one; we have no difficulty in believing this since the *Trois Vérités* and the *Discours Chrétiens* are the best proof of it. In the teaching of theology the still powerful *esprit de Sorbonne* had found a last refuge. The futile and endless argument the doctors of the Sorbonne indulged in would have come under the heading of the *pédantesque science* which we have found depicted on the title page of the *Sagesse*. The Renaissance had not yet touched this area of study, nor the teaching of medicine (and Molière gives us an exaggerated but true example of it) and Charron's critical opinion of the doctors of the Sorbonne is visible in some of his letters and in his *Petit Traicté de Sagesse.*

Back in Paris in late 1571, he began to preach by special appointment in the different parishes of Paris and his eloquent sermons soon made him famous. The qualities of his sermons were the same that were to make him a celebrated writer. His style was fluent, easy, clear, sober, and assured. It was a relief from the fashionable styles of the sermonizers of the time who indulged in exaggerated meta-

[9] Sabrié, *op. cit.*, p. 29.

phors and paraphrases, adding an occasional joke to relieve their dryness.

Charron's success brought him again as it had in Montpellier many invitations from many bishops to become "Chanoine avec bénéfices attachées" in their dioceses.[10] A learned and pious ecclesiastic who was also a patron of letters, Arnaus de Pontac, heard him preach at the Church of St. Paul in Paris in 1571 and was deeply impressed by Charron's sermons. When De Pontac became Bishop of Bazas (near Bordeaux) in 1572, he lost no time in prevailing upon Charron to join him in his new diocese.[11]

Arnaus de Pontac had studied languages and law in several French Universities. Just back from Rome, the young bishop with his humanistic and legal training must have been thoroughly acquainted with the counter-reform of the Council of Trent. We know that by that time the French bishops were endeavoring sincerely to apply the decrees of the Council, but they had to reckon with strong opposition. Arnaus de Pontac was from an old family of Bordeaux, and thus was able to foresee the difficulties he was to encounter in his new bishopric. He could not attempt alone to abide by the pope's orders and to enforce the decrees of the Council of Trent. We remember that Francis the First met with opposition every step of the way in his efforts to further the acceptance of Renaissance ideas in France. The conservatives' last refuge was the centuries-old rhetoric and ritual of the Faculties of Theology, and they doggedly maintained the intellectual supremacy of these outmoded forms. Their refusal to move along with their time and to correct antiquated usages which had become abusive or obsolete had become one of the main causes of the reformation movement and have made imperative the Catholic counter-reform. The Council of Trent was attempting to reform the physical body of the Church and to codify in the form of dogmas the part of the doctrine which had been misinterpreted. The Faculties of Theology had to be made to accept the latter without the benefit of an entertaining rhetorical debate.

---

[10] Charron, *De la Sagesse*, 1607, *Eloge*, p. 2: "...il s'acquit une merveilleuse réputation entre les plus doctes de ce temps là, mesmes à l'endroit de plusieurs Evesques et grands Prélats qui estoient lors en cette ville (Paris), et y avoit presse entre eux à qui le pourroit avoir en son Evesché ou Diocèse."

[11] Sabrié, *op. cit.*, p. 34.

We can understand that Arnaus de Pontac needed an able assistant, and Pierre Charron had all the necessary qualifications for this position. He had received formal training in the humanist tradition and had his doctorate in both canon and civil laws. His talent in the art of oratory was also a great asset, and Arnaus de Pontac made him his *théologal*. We have every reason to believe that the young bishop was satisfied with his choice because, as we have seen,[12] Charron seems to have been very successful in carrying out the necessary reforms in the seminaries where young clerks were trained for the priesthood. Furthermore this seems to have been one of the main concerns of the Pope at that time, and bishops were repeatedly instructed to watch over their schools.[13] It is certainly to be added to Pierre Charron's credit that he became successively *théologal* of Acqs, Lethourne, Agen, Cahors, and finally *écolâtre* in Bordeaux.

The decrees of the Council also controlled preaching, and Pierre Charron filled the position of *prédicateur ordinaire* in each of the dioceses mentioned above. His assignment was to correct the exaggerated taste in preaching which was more prevalent in the Southwest than anywhere else in France. He became the outstanding preacher of the Southwest and remained there for the next seventeen years.

La Rochemaillet is unhappily very brief on two points of great interest.[14] Charron was at one time a retainer of the Cardinal d'Armagnac, the papal legate in Avignon, but no date is given;[15] and again without much precision La Rochemaillet tells us that our young preacher was invited to the Court of Nérac to become the *prédicateur ordinaire* of Marguerite, Queen of Navarre, Duchess of Valois.

Nérac was then a haven of peace and of gentle and brilliant living in a war-shattered France. Besides Henri de Navarre and Marguerite, the Queen Mother, the princess Catherine de Navarre and the Marquis de Conti lived there from time to time. Many

---

[12] Supra, pp. 56 ff, and infra, p. 68 ff.

[13] Martin, *Gallicanisme*, pp. 96-116. Frangipani, the papal nuncio in Paris, writes on this matter continually. For instance, after the peace of St. Germain, favorable to the Huguenots on August 8, 1570, he insists again on the residence of the bishops, and on regular convocation of provincial synods for the instruction of the pastors, etc.

[14] Charron, *Sagesse*, 1607, p. 111.

[15] We have suggested one, 1569, the year Charron was away from Montpellier. This is also the time of Armagnac's move from Toulouse to Avignon.

illustrious visitors enhanced the reputation of the small court with their presence. Among them were Brantome, Guy de Pibrac, Michel de Montaigne, and Scaliger. Marguerite and her household went to mass in a chapel in the park, while Henri, his sister, and others of the *Eglise Réformée* went to listen to their Pastor's sermon. However, when Charron was there, Henri de Navarre went and listened to him (as La Rochemaillet tells us) and "s'est délecté et a pris plaisir extrême d'ouyr ses prédications". If he didn't convert Henri, Pierre Charron was at least able to charm him. Later our theologian-philosopher was to remember that period of his life in dedicating his *Trois Vérités* to Henri IV.

As early as 1576 the Chapter of St. André, Cathedral of Bordeaux, was interested in Charron and elected him *chanoine* on the 26th of August. Three days later, on the twenty-ninth, the Archbishop made him *écolâtre,* which was in this time of reform of the clergy a responsible position. Not only did he have the right to preach in the Cathedral and to teach theology, but he supervised all the schools of the diocese, including the seminary where the clerics were trained for priesthood.

Until he moved to Cahors in 1594 Bordeaux was his residence for eighteen years and so had managed to hold him longer than any other city. The capital of Guyenne was a good place for a humanist to reside. It was then one of the most brilliant cities in France; the Renaissance had made letters, poetry and erudition a daily subject of conversation and interest there.

Bordeaux was also the home of the College de Guyenne, one of the most active centers of humanism. Among others, Gronchy, Guérente, Mathurin Cordier, Vinet, and Buchanan had taught there. One of their alumni, Michel de Montaigne, was to become famous.

The nobility and the bourgeoisie followed the trend pioneered by the college, and Dezeimeris tells us that the city was turning into a vast academy where everyone was becoming so interested in the ancients that many, even among the ladies, were learning Greek.[16] Therefore Bordeaux offered to Charron a public capable of appreciating his talents and the inspiration to keep up with and develop his own cultural aspirations.

Although we do not know too much about his life there, Sabrié and Buffon have checked the records of the *Archives de la Gironde*

---

[16] Sabrié, *op. cit.,* p. 40, citing R. Dezeimeris, *De la Renaissance des Lettres à Bordeaux au XVI siècle,* Bordeaux: 1864.

and the public records of Angers and the *Bibliothèque Nationale* in Paris and were able to corroborate and even sometimes to add to what was known about him.[17]

A new source of information on the later part of Charron's life appeared when Louis Auvray discovered some letters from our canon to his friend La Rochemaillet.[18] Gabriel Naudé, a fervent admirer of Charron, had copied some of them, and his handwriting, according to Auvray, is recognizable. Naudé tells us that these letters were given to him to be copied by Gassendi, who had borrowed them from La Rochemaillet.

We know in general what the duties and responsibilities of our canon were during his stay in Bordeaux, but details are scarce. Sabrié found in the records of Bordeaux that on the second of April, 1576, the Parlament of the city had censured and put Charron on probation for libel uttered against the honor of the said court in some of his sermons.[19] No further facts are given. Sabrié thinks that Charron might have criticized the Parlement for too little action against the Huguenots. This is hard to believe since our canon never seems to have been sympathetic to radical action against the *Mouvement Réformé*. My belief is that it might have been caused by a quarrel over the jurisdiction of the Parlement over the clergy. Every time the Council of Trent was mentioned the Parlements would say, "Oui, mais sans préjudice des droits du Roi, ni des arrêts de la cour de Parlement". This had been a constant problem in the Gallican Church. The Concordat signed by Francis I had given the Crown and its Parlements more legal power but the Council of Trent had formally rescinded that order and jurisdiction over its own members was returned to the Church. As *écolâtre* Charron's own jurisdiction extended not only over all the bishop's schools but also over the younger canons. However, the Concordat was still the law, whereas the Council's decrees, not yet registered, were only a program for the clergy to follow.

Pierre Charron must have done his work well since the records show that in 1582 he was the delegate from the Chapter of Bordeaux

---

[17] We have mentioned these new finds of Sabrié and Bonnefon in Ch. I when we discussed the criticism on Charron. We will refer to these finds in this chapter as we come to them.

[18] Louis Auvray, "Lettres de Pierre Charron", *Revue d'Histoire Littéraire de la France*, Vol. I, Paris: Colin, 1894, p. 231.

[19] Sabrié, *op. cit.*, p. 41.

to the Provincial Council called in this city to fight the progress of heresy and maintain ecclesiastic discipline.

This Provincial Council, like other Provincial Councils, was called by the direct order of Henri III after the final session of the General Assembly of the French clergy in Melun in February, 1580. Arnaus de Pontac, bishop of Bazas, and Antoine Prevost de Sansac, archbishop of Bordeaux, both protectors of Charron, had been two of the most important leaders of the assembly. De Pontac addressed to the King the celebrated *Remontrance* in which he depicted the sad religious state of the kingdom of France.[20] Twenty-eight archiepiscopal sees and thousands of dioceses, monasteries, and vicarages were in the hands of laymen who enjoyed their revenue without carrying out the religious responsibilities attached to their posts. After he had obtained a yearly financial contribution of 1,350,000 francs from the clergy, the King had to promise the publication of the Council of Trent decrees at the earliest opportunity and thus give them power of law. Legal enforcement of the rulings of the Council decrees would then be possible and this was really the only remedy for the existing condition of simony. As a proof of good will, the King had asked for an immediate convocation of the provincial synods. The prime article on their agenda was to be the introduction of most of the decrees of the Council of Trent into their diocesan code.

Because, as we have seen, Charron's work in a position he held in his own diocese involved the application of the decrees of the Council of Trent, his appointment was more than fitting. Another delegate, François de Syrueilh, Archideacon of Blaye, tells us in his journal about the principal articles on the agenda of the synod:[21] residence, seminaries, recitation of divine services, and preaching. Charron had been working on these reforms since his appointments as *chantre, théologal,* and *écolâtre* in different dioceses of the southwest and finally in Bordeaux.[22]

With the playing of a comedy in Latin by some students, the activities of the Council ended on a note consonant with the humanistic tradition and with the Council's duties. We know that in Renaissance France writing and producing Latin plays was in great favor. Some of these plays written by college professors were regular tragedies,

---

[20] Martin, *Gallicanisme,* pp. 151 f.

[21] Sabrié, *op. cit.,* p. 42.

[22] Supra, p. 56 ff.

introducing the age of the French classical tragedy that was just developing. Most often however, they were only small plays *de circonstance,* as is the case here. This play showed in essence that although in the past benefice-holders had not always done their duty, nevertheless at the present time many well-educated and able men were serving their charges well. We do not know the author of the play, but Pierre Charron was the *écolâtre* and might have had a hand in it. If so, the play was a compliment to those in attendance, because it conformed to the new program and the new rulings of which our *écolâtre* had charge. On the other hand, if he didn't write this play, then we can consider it a compliment paid to him for a job well done. For us this is one more proof that the *Bordelais* had not waited for Henri III's order to begin observing most of the decrees of the Council of Trent, even if those decrees were not official laws of the kingdom.

We find a last official mention of Charron's presence in Bordeaux in 1588. On the 25th of June our canon, again an official delegate of his chapter, brought the city officials the sum of three hundred pounds as a contribution of the Cathedral chapter to help defray the great expenses incurred by the plague of 1585.

This period of Charron's residence in Bordeaux is also important to his biographers since it is somewhere in the 1580's that they place the first meeting of our canon with Montaigne. The two men probably met for the first time at the Provincial Council.

Yet we cannot be sure that it was the first time; they certainly could have met before. Montaigne had been elected Mayor of Bordeaux on the first of August, 1581. He had been traveling almost constantly since 1579; but from 1571 to 1579 Montaigne and Charron were both in and out of Bordeaux, and could easily have met. Furthermore, as we have already mentioned, Montaigne had been a guest at the Court of Nerac several times, and Pierre Charron had been at the same court as *prédicateur ordinaire.*

Sabrié and Bonnefon agree that the 1580's saw a closer acquaintance between the new mayor of Bordeaux and our *écolâtre.* This position called for continuous contact with the civil authorities. Later, at the time of the Provincial Council, we find another occasion on which the two men might have become better acquainted.

Both men were becoming famous. The *Essays* had made Montaigne known not only in Bordeaux, where Millanges was printing them, but all over the province of Guyenne, and in Paris and other intellectual centers which were never lagging too far behind. Charron was the outstanding preacher of the Southwest and was already known and esteemed in other parts of France. We find mention in his letters of invitations from many bishops to come and preach, and we find in the records that wherever he went in his travels, even on business, he was asked to preach. We will see later that at the time of his trip to Paris, where he went to seek entrance into a *Célestin* or *Chartreux* monastery, he stopped in Saintes and Angers to preach and later to deliver the Lenten sermons in Paris and in Angers.[23]

The Provincial Council of 1582 in Bordeaux provided a new occasion for Montaigne and Charron to exchange views and to discuss the great distress and anguish caused in their hearts by the civil war and the religious divisions of their country.

This troubled period[24] had already witnessed many atrocities on both sides and was to witness the assassination of the Guises and later of Henry III. Both Charron and Montaigne saw, as one always does during troubled periods, the worst instincts of men come to the surface. There were excesses everywhere: intense people could no longer distinguish between their religion and their religious passions, crimes were committed by both sides in the name of religion, and politicians leaned indifferently to either side in order to obtain their ends.

The first absolute proof that the relationship of the two men was more than one of mere acquaintance is the gift of a copy of the *Catéchisme*[25] of Bernardino Ochino to our canon by the author of the *Essays* in his castle of Montaigne, on the second of July, 1586.

Bonnefon[26] sees in this gift a proof only of the liberal thought of the two friends, and of the high esteem in which they held one another. Sabrié commits himself even less: "Singulier cadeau que Montaigne faisait là à son ami le Chanoine de St. André".[27]

As a matter of fact, it must have been a rather disturbing *Catéchisme*. Bernardino Ochino, the author, was ousted from Zurich and Bâle because of it. Ochino was a former general of the *Capucin* order and a remarkable preacher, renowned for his zealous and

---

[23] Charron, *Sagesse,* 1607, p. 5.

[24] See Chapter III.

[25] This copy is at the Bibliothèque Nationale. It has the signatures of both Montaigne and Charron with the inscription "Ex dono dicti domini de Montaigne in suo Castello, 2 Julii 1586".

[26] Bonnefon, *op. cit.,* p. 227.

[27] Sabrié, *op. cit.,* p. 45.

austere character. He had joined Calvin and later had helped Cranmer organize the second reform in England in 1547.

However, Montaigne and Charron were both intelligent and reflective men who had studied the conditions and needs of their age, penetrating far beneath the surface. They were both striving to find the solution for the troubles of their time, and, because of the frequent meetings of the two writers during the Provincial Council in Bordeaux, one can certainly assume that they had discussed the problems of the reform. They had met and worked together, one as the King's representative, the other as the Church's representative. They must have met many sincere people, and must have been concerned with their honest perplexities on religious matters. Reform literature had flooded France for half a century and the *Catéchisme* was one of the most violently disputed items. Could we venture to suppose that in giving Charron this catechism Montaigne was suggesting to the lawyer-theologian that he needed to know his adversaries better in order to fight them on their own ground?

We may surmise from this that Charron was slowly beginning to see the need for an apologetic of the Catholic faith and for the reconciliation of religious faith and human wisdom in the same doctrine. The events of the years through which our canon lived could not help but increase these convictions.

Toward the end of 1588 Charron left Bordeaux for Paris, not planning to return. In accordance with the decrees of the Council of Trent, which he had helped to uphold, he had asked the Holy See for the authority to exchange his positions of *chantre* and *écolâtre* at Bordeaux for the identical positions then held by Henri des Aigues at Condom.[28]

Pierre Charron had decided that his sermons and his teaching needed to be supplemented by some writing and publishing. It is amazing to see that, although the pamphlets and treatises of the reform had been answered from the pulpit, there were few published Catholic works that refuted adequately the Protestant propaganda blasts.

In Charron's mind the post at Condom was to be a temporary arrangement which would give him more time for writing than he had had before. He hoped eventually to be admitted either at the

---

[28] Bonnefon, *op. cit.*, p. 229; Sabrié, *op. cit.*, p. 53. They both refer to: Chanoine Allain, *Inventaire Sommaire des Archives de l'archeveché de Bordeaux antérieures à 1789*, Bordeaux: 1803, p. 298.

Carthusian or the Celestinian monastery in Paris. La Rochemaillet[29] tells us that he liked solitude, that he had taken a vow to become a Carthusian monk, and that he came to Paris to seek admission into the order's monastery there. He reached the capital at the time of the *Etats de Blois* after having stopped over in Saintes and in Angers where he delivered sermons.

As I have already said,[30] Charron's position and intellectual attitude in his own period have always been neglected, and a picture of Charron as a disciple of Montaigne has been constantly present in the mind of his critics. It is therefore understandable that La Rochemaillet's reason for Pierre Charron's' taking vows does not satisfy any of them, and all of our *théologal's* biographers are quite intrigued and quite disturbed by Charron's decision, as monasteries, in their minds, are in conflict with ideals of a disciple of Montaigne. Critics are also very much disturbed by some of Charron's reactions at the height of the League movement (as we will see later), and they attempt to explain his apparent inconsistency by dividing Charron's life into two periods separated by the year 1589. Before 1589 Charron is (according to these biographers) the preacher and a simple acquaintance of Montaigne. After 1589, following the period of his sermons for the League, and because the Carthusians and the *Célestins* had refused him entrance into their monasteries, Pierre Charron, according to his critics, suddenly decided to direct his life to an entirely different path. Abandoning all his previous ideals and the religious undertakings which had produced his celebrated *Discours Chrétiens* and which had led him to the gates of a convent, our canon is supposed to have turned suddenly into a half-pagan philosopher, to have been converted to the philosophy of Montaigne and become his disciple. This is to introduce too many complications, while disregarding the facts of Charron's life and the fact that the *Trois Vérités* was published in 1593, four years after this so-called about-face. And the *Trois Vérités* (as we will see) is certainly in the spirit of the years preceding 1589. The elaborate and shaky hypothesis presupposing a *volte-face* for Charron in 1589 would be unnecessary if his critics did not want to see in the author of the *Sagesse* a disciple of Montaigne. On the contrary the study of Charron's life as we are conducting it now will show before and after 1589 a continuity of purpose fitting to his ministry.

---

29 Charron, *Sagèsse*, 1607, *Eloge*, p. V.

30 Supra, pp. 15 ff.

Sabrié does not agree with the critics who preceded him and does not see any radical change in Charron's character after 1589, nor any radical change in the friendship of the two writers. He also points out that Montaigne was more religious than many are led to believe. In Italy he had offered to Our Lady of Lorette a silver engraving representing himself, his wife and his daughter kneeling in front of the Virgin; and when he had bad attacks of gravel he received the last sacraments and placed himself and his soul in the hands of God or nature.[31] For Montaigne and for Charron, nature was synonymous with the force of creation in the order desired by the Creator; it was the expression of the divine will in the order of the world surrounding us. This is apparent in many places: for instance, in the second preface of the *Sagesse* where Charron, speaking of the guidance the mind of man should follow, said, "...se réglant en toute choses selon nature, c'est à dire la raison première et universelle loy et lumière inspirée de Dieu, et qui esclaire en nous,..."[32] Sabrié states also that he is not too sure that Montaigne would have blamed Charron for having "put a foot into the League"[33] as our canon admits he did, or "for having yearned for the solitude of the monastery". But the question of why Charron wanted to enter a monastery is still a problem.

One can suggest a simple explanation for the canon's taking vows. La Rochemaillet tells us that his friend had taken a vow to become a *Chartreux*.[34] The great plague which had afflicted Bordeaux in 1585 was still fresh in everyone's memory and Charron, before leaving that city, had taken care of the last details relative to the epidemic,[35] one of the most ravaging of the century in the Bordeaux area. Charron could have very well taken a vow to become a *Chartreux* on the condition that he live through the plague.

It could not have been that he feared death, since in his testament and in his last words we have proof that he was ready to accept death at any time. But one does feel that he had reached a turning point in his life. As I have already stated, he felt that his preaching and the work of the counter-reform needed to be supplemented by pertinent writing answering the many honest perplexities of sincere persons concerned with religious matters. By that time

---

[31] Sabrié, *op. cit.*, pp. 51 f.
[32] Charron, *Sagesse,* 1607, preface, p. 8.
[33] Bonnefon, *op. cit.*, p. 235
[34] Charron, *Sagesse,* 1607, *Eloge,* p. V.
[35] Supra. p. 69.

the *Trois Vérités* must have been in the making. Pierre Charron wanted to live long enough to see his work through, and a Carthusian or Celestinian monastery may have seemed the right place for a religious life and the pursuit of his program of apologetics.

Some of his critics have maliciously suggested that Charron would not have given up too much if he had succeeded in his monastic desire since life in many monasteries at the time of the Renaissance seems to have been rather worldly and not unlike Rabelais' *Abbaye de Thélème.*[36] But the two monasteries Charron had chosen had good reputations and the Cardinal Alexandro de Medici, reporting to the Pope at the time of the peace of Vervins, praised the Carthusians and the Augustinians for following "regulations" and for their good behavior.[37]

However, as we have seen,[38] before he got to Paris to try to enter a monastery, he interrupted his trip to deliver a series of sermons at Saintes, Angers and other places, and his arrival in the capital was delayed for a long time.

The political situation was very tense at this moment; bishops and nobles were trying to influence public opinion by all possible means. One of the best of these means was good preaching. The *Etats Généraux* were just opening in Blois, and we do not know whether Charron was there or not.[39] But we do know that his preaching was so popular that certain churches were too small to accomodate the people who came to listen to him.[40]

Finally he went to Paris to see about being admitted to one of the monasteries, and since the answer seems to have been reserved, he returned to Angers for further preaching, leaving to his friend La Rochemaillet the task of finding out the answer for him. Charron wrote him repeatedly, insisting over and over again that La Rochemaillet obtain a positive answer for him.[41]

---

[36] Bonnefon, *op. cit.,* p. 238.

[37] Lavisse, *op. cit.,* Vol. VII, p. 90.

[38] Supra, pp. 72 f.

[39] He signed in 1596 the "compte de la recepte géneralle des decomes ordinaires payables en l'annee 1588", and "Compte particulier des frais du voyage et retour de messieurs les prelatz et depputez du Clergé assemblez en corps d'Estat dans la ville de Bloys, en l'annee 1588". Bonnefon, *op. cit.,* p. 231.

[40] Louis Auvray, *op. cit.,* p. 308, quoting Journal de Jehan Louvet, Revue de l'Anjou et du Maine et Loire 3eme Année, tome II, 1854, pp. 137-161.

[41] *Ibid.,* p. 308.

But Pierre Charron was not accepted in either monastery; we do not know why. His biographers try to explain this refusal by considering his age, which might have made adjustment to monastic life difficult, or by intimating that such a sudden and unexplained change in his career, until then quite successful, would have seemed suspect.

As we have already seen, Charron probably renounced his preaching and his successful administrative career, not to become a monk but to become a writer. The numerous duties of his position in Bordeaux did not give him enough leisure and he accepted the quieter canonicate of Condom as a place to take refuge if his other plans failed.

We should not be amazed, as his biographers are, to see him seeking the peace and serenity of the cloister. Bonnefon, for instance, thinks that a disciple of Montaigne should not have been interested in monasteries but should have followed the example of the master by withdrawing to the country.[42] We have already discussed this, but we should add that the Carthusian monks lived in isolated small *pavillons* or chalets grouped around a cloister, an environment as private as Montaigne's retreat; furthermore, there was no worry about the basic necessities of life.

After the two orders had refused to accept him, Charron was relieved of his vow.[43] But he was still in Angers in February, 1589. Indignant, as were many other Frenchmen after the murder of the Duke of Guise, he leaned toward the League, and his preaching became so partisan that the Duke d'Aumont had him suspended when he took possession of the city. But Charron was never entirely in sympathy with the League. He tells us himself "un temps a été que je marchandais être de la Ligue et y ai mis un pied dedans",[44] and after the ban against him had been lifted he reversed his position and reminded people of the divine right of royalty.

Pierre Charron's biographers, Sabrié excepted, have criticised him for his participation in the League and for his apparent lack of self-control. They did not know that Charron had been a prisoner

[42] Bonnefon, *op. cit.*, p. 236.

[43] Charron, *Sagesse*, 1607, *Eloge*, p. V, "Il fut assuré par Faber doyen de la Sorbonne, Tyrius, jesuite écossais, et Feuardent, Cordelier, très doctes théologiens, qu'en conscience il était quitte d'un tel voeu...".

[44] Bonnefon, *op. cit.*, p. 235, quoting the "Lettre à un Docteur de Sorbonne Avril 1589, Qu'il n'est permis, ni loisible à un sujet, pour quelque cause et raison que ce soit, de se liguer, bander et rebeller contre son roi".

of the Protestants twelve years before when they had taken Montpellier after a long siege. They also forget that the assassination of the Cardinal de Guise, the first prelate of the Church of France, was not only a political assassination but a terrible sacrilege capable of inflaming the wrath of all those close to the Church. They saw in the cardinal a martyr, not simply a politician who had lost. Pierre Charron had to take sides, at least for a while, and Sabrié agrees on this. He even cites the *Essays* to show that Montaigne would not have blamed his friend:

> De se tenir chancelant et mestic, de tenir son affection immobile et sans inclination aux troubles de son pays et en une division publique, je ne le trouve ny beau ny honneste; il faut prendre party.

Charron regained his intellectual balance and avoided hysterical excesses. In a letter to La Rochemaillet dated March 10, 1589, he mentions two pamphlets: the first, a League pamphlet against the King which he finds well-written but too violent in tone; the second, the King's declaration against M. du Maine which he finds well-constructed but full of deliberate lies.[46] He tells La Rochemaillet that although the interdiction against his preaching has been lifted, he is still confined to Angers and is anxious to leave.[47] A little later he tells how he is afflicted by the public agitation and how much he would like to withdraw somewhere into isolation.[48]

Finally, at the end of August 1589, Charron went back to Bordeaux, where he met Montaigne again. La Rochemaillet tells us about their close friendship and how devoted they were to each other.[49] Except for that vague mention, however, we have no information from either Montaigne or Charron concerning their relationship. We know that Montaigne must have held him in esteem or he would not have given Charron his copy of the Ochino ca-

---

[45] Sabrié, *op, cit.*, p. 51.

[46] Auvray, *op. cit.*, p. 308, Lettre V, D'Angers, X Mars, 1589: "...Le Martyre est assez bien fait mais trop injurieus. Je juge que M. Puginat l'a fait. La Declaration du Roy contre de Maine bien faicte, mais pleine de menteries grossières et impostures que les Chambrières y voient,...".

[47] *Ibid.*, D'Angers, 12 Mai: "...J'ai été inhibité de prescher et mis à l'arrest par la ville... j'ai permission maintenant de prescher et fus restitué en chaire jour de l'Ascencion, mais l'arrest dure encore...".

[48] *Ibid.*, Lettre D'Angers 1er Juillet, 1589.

[49] Charron, Sagesse, 1607, Eloge, p. VI.

techism, which even at that time was very valuable, especially to a bibliophile like Montaigne. Later the author of the *Essays* was to will his friend the right to wear his "Coat of Arms", a great proof of friendship and trust, since we know that Montaigne was very proud of his nobility.

It is probable that Montaigne was familiar with the contents of the *Trois Vérités*. It was to be the first published work of Charron and it paralleled the effort of the author of the *Essays*, who had tried to make himself (and in turn his readers) aware of the human heritage of their civilization. Charron wanted his readers to become aware of the religious heritage of their forefathers; and he chose to do this through theology, but by relying also upon the senses and reason. Montaigne,[50] like Sebonde, had tried to do this in order to show the need of a higher doctrine that would amend the weakness of human reason. Charron did it, and did it well, in his *Trois Vérités*. We find there the "Pari de Pascal", and when Pascal used the same argument, and spoke from his heart instead of from his head, he had even greater success.

The *Trois Vérités*[51] was published in Bordeaux in 1593. This polemical and dogmatic work had such success that many counterfeit editions appeared in Paris, Lyons, and Brussels. Pierre Charron had not signed his work and pirated editions were common. The Brussels edition (1595) was published under the name of Benoist Vaillant, a lawyer of Sainte Foy.[52]

The statement contained in the third *Vérité* that the Catholic Church was superior to all the schismatic churches provoked an angry response from the Protestants. According to Brunet's *Manuel du Libraire*, this anonymous answer was published in La Rochelle in 1594.[53]

The bishop of Cahors, Antoine d'Hébrard de Saint Sulpice, a great humanist and a friend of letters, was one of the most distinguished of Charron's protectors. According to Sabrié, Antoine d'Hébrard was appreciated not only in France but even in Rome in the best of humanist circles.[54] The Pope and the Sacred College were delighted to see in such a young prelate the seriousness, wis-

---

50 Michel de Montaigne, *Essais*, Pierre Villey, Paris: Alcan, 1922, II, 12.

51 Supra, p. 22.

52 Bonnefon, *op. cit.*, pp. 250-251.

53 *Response à un livre nouvellement mis en lumière* intitulé les *Trois Véritéz*, Supra, p. 15.

54 Bonnefon, *op. cit.*, pp. 250 f.

LA
REPLIQVE
MAISTRE
CHARRON, SVR
ONCE FAITE A SA
troisiesme Verité cy deuant
Imprimée à la Rochelle.

Auec vne table fort ample des matieres contenues en ladite troisiesme Verité.

A PARIS.

Chez Estienne vallet, ruë des sept voyes, deuant le College de Rhetms, à la Byble d'or.

M. D. XCV.

LA
REPLIQVE
DE MAISTRE
PIERRE LE CHARRON,
SVR LA RESPONCE FAITE
à sa troisiesme Verité cy
deuant imprimée a
la Rochelle

Auec vne table fort ample des matieres contenues en ladite troisiesme Verité.

A LYON.
PAR IEAN DIDIER.

1 6 9 5.

LA
REPLIQVE
DE MAISTRE
PIERRE LE CHARRON,
SVR LA RESPONCE FAITE
à sa troisiesme Verité cy
deuant imprimée à
la Rochelle:

Auec vne table fort ample des matieres contenues en ladite troisiesme Verité.

A LYON.
PAR IEAN DIDIER.

1 5 9 6.

LA
REPLIQVE
DE MAISTRE
IEAN LE CHARRON,
SVR LA RESPONSE
faicte à sa III. Verité, cy-deuant
Imprimée à la Rochelle.

Auec vne table fort ample des matieres contenuës en ladite troisiesme Verité.

A PARIS,

Chez ROBERT BERTAVLT, au mont S. Hilaire, à l'Estoille couronnee.

M. DC. XXV.

dom and scholarship found ordinarily only among the oldest of the Church's distinguished humanists.

It was therefore a great honor for Charron to be asked to come to Cahors as a *théologal* in 1594. He was already a canon of this cathedral, as he was of several others in the Southwest, but he had no charge requiring residence. We can imply from this that he was also canon and *chantre* in Condom but was not yet *théologal* there.

D'Hébrard de Saint Sulpice had been very much impressed by the *Trois Vérités* and was anxious to know its author. It seems that Quercy had been greatly tried by the religious wars and that its clergy was in dire need of the salutary reforms of the Council of Trent. There were no schools or seminaries there, and the good bishop had to have his instructions to his clergy translated from Latin into French so that they could understand them clearly.

The University was reopened by *lettres patentes* from the King, and Pierre Charron probably taught there in 1595 when he assumed his charge. Sabrié thinks that the *Discours Chrétiens* may be composed of material from his theology classes.[55] Among his many tasks, our canon prepared there his second edition of the *Trois Vérités*. He had delayed its publication long enough to prepare answers to the new arguments presented by the Protestants.

This "seconde edition revüe, corrigée et de beaucoup augmentée" appeared in Bordeaux in 1595.[56] The Protestants felt that they had to answer again, but this time through one of their most able theologians, François du Jon.[57]

At this point, Charron reached the conviction that a third edition of the *Trois Vérités* would not provide an effective answer to Du Jon and other less well known polemists.[58] Instead, he turned all of his energy to the preparation of *De la Sagesse* which he intended

---

[55] Sabrié, *op. cit.*, p. 78.

[56] The third *Vérité* has a separate title *La Vérité troisième, de toutes les parts qui sont en la Chretiensté, la Catholique romaine est la meilleure, contre tous hérétiques et schismatiques,* Au Roy à Bourdeaus: par S. Millanges, 1595.

It was followed by Charron's answer to his critics. This answer has often been printed alone in pirated editions: *La Réplique de Maistre Pierre Le Charron sur la Reponse faicte à la Troisesme Vérité cy devant imprimée à la Rochelle,* Lyon: Jean Didier, 1595.

[57] Supra, p. 24.

[58] Jean Gardesy, *Epistola Johannis Gardesii montalbaneusis ad Petrum Charronium parisiensem,* Montalban: Haultin, 1597.

For other polemists see supra, p. 23 ff.

to be the foundation-stone for his work justifying the Catholic point of view.[59]

Just after the publication of the second edition of the *Trois Vérités,* Charron was chosen representative of the province of Bordeaux to the general assembly of the clergy of France, which was to meet in Paris at the monastery of the Augustinians on the sixth of November, 1595. Not only had Charron received the high honor of representing his province, but he was also elected the first secretary of the assembly. We believe we can see in this appointment a recognition of the outstanding work of our canon in applying the decrees of the Council of Trent in the Southwest.

Two of the main concerns of the assembly were the application of these decrees and the finding of remedies to stop the mishandling of church benefices by the royal power. Henri IV promised to abide by the new decrees, as Henri III had done,[60] but soon thereafter he nominated a four-year-old boy, Charles de Lévis, as bishop of Lodève.

Taking advantage of the stay of Charron in Paris, the Rector of St. Eustache invited him to deliver the All Saints' Day and the Lenten sermons in 1595 and 1596. By the end of 1596, after having signed and sent to Rome the minutes of the Assembly, Pierre Charron went back to Cahors and gave to his new project, the *Sagesse,* all the time he could spare from his absorbing duties as *Chanoine Vicaire Général.*[61]

Our canon was modest and in his letter to La Rochemaillet the statement "Et Monseigneur qui me charge sur les espaules tout le soin de son clergé!" does not tell his friend that he had been promoted to the rank of *Vicaire Général* by the distinguished bishop. Mr. Sabrié found proof of that new dignity in official documents of the Cathedral of Cahors.[62] It was a high honor for Charron, since this appointment was usually the last step before elevation to a bishop's seat. To be the *Vicaire Général* of Hébrard de Saint Sulpice made it a double honor.

---

[59] Auvray, *op. cit.,* p. 308, *Lettre à La Rochemaillet De Cahors,* 8 Mars, 1597.

[60] Supra, p. 68.

[61] Auvray, *op. cit.,* p. 308, *Lettre à La Rochemaillet De Cahors,* 4 Septembre 1596", "... je n'ai point encore eu le loisir d'écrire, tant j'ai trouve ici de besogne taillée; et Monseigneur qui me charge sur les espaules tout le soin de son clergé!".

[62] Sabrié, *op. cit.,* p. 89.

The *Sagesse* was behind schedule, as the letters to La Rochemaillet show. By 1600 however, it was almost ready for publication. During the year 1600, Charron made strenuous efforts to obtain royal *privilèges* for the publication of all his works, including the *Sagesse*. These efforts were crowned with success and the new edition came off the S. Millanges press[63] in June, 1601.

Our canon did not seem satisfied with his life in Cahors. His letters to La Rochemaillet show a deep desire to leave Quercy where he had few friends outside of his protector. The high position he had achieved there did not seem to alter his desire for a change. He also had many offers from bishops from more northern regions, among them Bishop Miron of Angers. But our preacher-philosopher declined them all and decided in favor of retirement in the warmer Southwest.[64] By the exchange of benefices made in 1588 we know that he liked Condom, and that the offer of the charge of *théologal* made the little city even more attractive. On the sixth of May, 1600, Charron moved to Condom.

La Rochemaillet tells us in his *Eloge* that Charron had a comfortable and nicely furnished house built so that he could live and entertain his friends there. He was then fifty-nine and at that age in sixteenth century France, traveling and moving about was quite an ordeal or even sometimes almost impossible. Charron should not be called an epicurean, as Garasse and other critics have called him because he tried to prepare himself for old age and to minimize its effects; on the contrary he should be commended for resigning himself finally to a sedentary life and trying to make the most of it. It shouldn't have been too hard a task. At that time Jean du Chemin, a poet and a humanist, was Bishop of Condom; and Gérard-Marie Imbert, a poet and a distinguished Hellenist, was a member of the Chapter; a few years before, Du Bartas, the author of the *Semaines*, had lived there. Charron was in congenial company.

In October, 1600 he published a collection of his sermons known as *Discours Chrétiens*.[65] He seems to have enjoyed life in this little

---

[63] Pierre Le Charron, *De la Sagesse*, Bourdeaux: S. Millanges, 1601.

[64] Auvray, *op. cit.*, p. 321.

[65] In two parts. The first, dedicated to the Cardinal de Sourlis, Archevecque de Bordeaux, has for title: *L'Octave contenant huict discours du Saint Sacrement avec un autre discours de la Communion des Saints*, par M. Pierre Charron, Parisien, A Bourdeaus par S. Millanges imprimeur ordinaire du Roy, 1600. The second is: *Discours Chretiens*, de M. Pierre Charron,

southern province and wanted his good friend De la Rochemaillet to come and join him. He wrote him often, and it is through these letters[66] that we obtain much information concerning Charron's feelings at this time.

In a letter from Condom, dated June 10, 1602, Charron told La Rochemaillet that he knew that his *Sagesse* had been variously understood by different people. Several things were said rather boldly, he tells his friend, and he therefore reviewed and corrected it and in several places softened his arguments somewhat.

Our philosopher knew the Sorbonne, and he tried to anticipate its action by changing a few things for the new edition of his work. Furthermore, he made every effort to obtain an advance approval[67] from two doctors of the Sorbonne before the work was published in Paris. More changes seemed to come to his mind and he decided to go to Paris to watch over the publication himself. It was there on Sunday, November 16, 1603, that Pierre Charron died of a stroke without having completed the second edition of his *Sagesse*. His good friend La Rochemaillet finished it for him, overcoming all obstacles, political and religious, that the doctors of the Sorbonne tried to raise.

Two new editions of the *Sagesse* appeared in 1604[68] and 1607.[69] In 1604 there appeared a new edition of the *Discours Chrétiens*[70] to which the *Divinité* had been added; and finally in 1606 Pierre Charron's little pamphlet *Traité de Sagesse* came out.[71]

But death had not found our *chanoine théologal* unprepared. He had written a will on January 30, 1602[72] wherein he had dis-

---

Seconde Partie, A Bourdeaus par Simon Millanges, 1601, and is dedicated to his new bishop: Jean du Chemin.

[66] Auvray, *op. cit.*, p. 308, "Lettres de Pierre Charron à Gabriel Michel de la Rochemaillet".

[67] *Ibid.*, Letter of January 12, 1603.

[68] *De la Sagesse, trois livres,* par Pierre Charron, Parisien Docteur ès droicts, Seconde edition revüe et augmentée, A Paris: chez David Douceur, 1604.

[69] *De la Sagesse, trois livres,* par Pierre Charron, Parisién docteur ès-droicts. Dernière Edition, en laquelle pour le contentement du curieux lecteur a esté adjousté à la fin tout ce qui pouvait avoir été retranché aux précédentes impressions, ...

[70] *Discours chrestiens de la divinité, création, rédemption et octave du Saint Sacrement* par M. Pierre Charron, Parisien, docteur, théologal Paris, Pierre Bertault, 1604.

[71] *Traicté de Sagesse,* composé par Pierre Charron, Parisien, docteur ès droits, ... Paris, David Le Clerc, 1606.

[72] Bonnefon, *op. cit.*, pp. 308-311. He refers us also to *Archives histo-*

DE LA SAGESSE TROIS LIVRES,

PAR

PIERRE CHARRON PARISIEN,
Docteur és Droicts.

DERNIERE EDITION,

En laquelle, pour le contentement du curieux Lecteur, a esté adiousté à la fin tout ce qui pouuoit auoir esté retranché aux precedentes impressions.

PLVS

Vn Eloge veritable, ou sommaire de la vie de l'Autheur, l'Explication de la figure qui est au frontispice du present liure, auec vne table des matieres principales y contenues.

A PARIS,
Chez DAVID DOVCEVR, Libraire Iuré, ruë Sainct Iaques, au Mercure arresté.
M. DCVII.
Auec priuilege du Roy.

posed of his possessions. Montaigne's brother-in-law was the executor of the will. His wife. Léonore de Montaigne, received five hundred *écus*. Many of his friends, the Hospital of Condom, and the poor had their share. Charron was one of the first men of our modern age to establish a fund for poor young men and women, through which the young men would receive scholarships to continue their studies, and the young women dowries so that they could marry honorably.

Mr. Bonnefon tells us that we do not know much about what happened to that trust fund up to 1647. But through records of the *Archives de la Gironde* he was able to discover that from 1647 to 1734, three hundred and thirty-one girls received dowries ranging from fifteen to one hundred and fifty pounds. As for the scholarships, records were found only from 1655 to 1711, and that account was poorly kept. However, that does not diminish the kindness and thoughtfulness of Charron's gesture.

A careful study of the life and the responsibilities of our canon has shown that he has a rather impressive stature for a "petit disciple de Montaigne". After an excellent humanistic education Charron entered the service of the Church and secured a doctorate in canon and civil law. Soon he achieved a nation-wide fame for his talents as a preacher, and great honors and responsibilities were bestowed upon him. His influence and his responsibility in the application of the decrees of the Council of Trent in the dioceses of the southwest can hardly be denied. He was raised to the very high post of *Vicaire Général* and was chosen as a representative to the Provincial Council and to the general assembly of the clergy of 1595 where he received the great honor of being elected First Secretary of the Assembly. Then Pierre Charron began to write, and his very successful treatises, which we are going to study now, added to his fame.

---

riques de la Gironde, t. XVIII, pp. 463-472, and t. XXIV, pp. 229. Charron's bequest says: "Je donne, lègue et laisse aux pauvres écoliers et pauvres filles à marier la somme de deux mille quatre cents écus, laquelle somme sera mise en bonnes et assurées mains, à raison du denier douze, ... et que la moitié du revenu de la dite somme, qui est cent écus soit employée à l'entretènement de trois ou quatre ou cinz pauvres enfants aux études, lesquels seront choisis par mes dits héritiers et exécuteurs et entretenus trois ou quatre ou cinq années... et l'autre moitié du revenu qui est aussi cent écus, sera employée à marier tous les ans trois ou quatre ou cinq pauvres filles".

Chapter V

THE WORKS OF CHARRON

The first published work of Pierre Charron, *Les Trois Vérités,*[1] is a treatise of apologetics for the Catholic faith and a polemic against its detractors.

Until that time most of the apologetics of the Catholic Church and the answers to Protestant treatises had been written in Latin and were consequently beyond the reach and understanding of the average man; among them were those of Cheffonds, Bellarmin, Hosius, and Cousin.[2]

It is easy to understand that, after twenty-three years of experience as a preacher, our canon would want to put in writing the developments of the dogma and the defenses of it which he had probably given so often from the pulpit.

Charron wanted truth to reach every man and wanted to demonstrate to each the three fundamental truths or *vérités*:

1 That God exists and religion is necessary.

2 That there is a "revealed religion"; that it is the Chris-

[1] Pierre Charron, *Les Trois Véritéz contre les athées, idolâtres, juifs, mahumétans, hérétiques et schismatiquès, le tout traicté en trois livres,* Bourdeaux: Millanges, 1593, 2d ed., 1595.

[2] Hosius, *Opera,* Cologne: 1584.

———, *Confessio catholica fidei christianae vèl explicatio quaedam confessionis factae in synodo provinciali habiita Petrikoviae anno 1551,* Mayence: 1557.

Christophe de Cheffonds, *Novae illustrationis christianae fidei adversus impios, libertinos, atheos, epicureos et omne genus infideles,* Paris: 1586.

Jean Cousin, *Fundamenta rèligionis, hoc est, tractatus de naturali Dei cognitione, de animi immortalitate et de justitia Dei adversus politicorum seu atheorum errores,* Duaci: 1597.

LES
TROIS VERITEZ
CONTRE LES ATHEES,
IDOLATRES, IVIFS, MAHVMETANS, Heretiques, & Schismatiques. Le tout traicté en trois liures.

Auec l'indice des principales matieres.

A BOVRDEAVS,
Par S. MILLANGES Imprimeur ordinaire du Roy.
M.D. XCIII.

LES
TROIS VERITEZ
CONTRE TOVS ATHEES,
[IDOLA]TRES, IVIFS, [Mahum]etans, Heretiques, [&] Schismatiques.

Le tout traicté en trois liures.

AVEC L'INDICE DES PRINCIPALES MATIERES.

Reueu, corrigé, & augmenté de nouueau.

A PARIS,
Chez LEGER DELAS rue Sainct Iacques au Soleil d'Or.
M. D. XCIIII.

LES
TROIS VERITEZ
SECONDE EDITION
reueüe, corrigée, & de beaucoup augmentée,

Auec vn aduertissement & bref examen sur la Response faicte à la troisiesme verité, de nouueau imprimée à la Rochelle.

Par M. PIERRE le CHARRON Parisien.

A BOVRDEAVS,
Par S. MILLANGES Imprimeur ordinaire du Roy.
1595.
Auec Priuilege du Roy.

LES
TROIS VERITEZ CONTRE TOVS
ATHEES, IDOLATRES, Iuifs, Mahumetans, Heretiques, & Schismatiques.

Le tout traicté en trois liures.

AVEC L'INDICE DES principales matieres.

Reueu, corrigé, & augmété de nouueau

A PARIS,
Chez Iean du Carroy Imprimeur, au mont S Hylaire en la maison de Coquetel.
M. D. XCV.

tian religion; and that Christ, the Son of God, is its founder.

3 That among the Christian religions, Catholicism, the oldest, is the only religion that keeps the truth pure.

Most of Charron's critics dispose of the *Trois Vérités* as a polemical treatise directed against the Protestants, one in which our canon refutes the *Traité de l'Eglise* of Duplessis-Mornay.[3] Their attitude towards the *Trois Vérités* is in my mind an additional proof showing how much the critics of our canon were bent on following the already set pattern for the evaluation of Pierre Charron's works: the *Trois Vérités* is a work of apologetics for the Catholic Church and of polemic against her enemies and therefore would hardly fit into the general plan of making of Pierre Charron the "Patriarche des esprits forts" as he has so often been called since Garasse gave him this title.

It should also be noted that the preface of the *Trois Vérités* throws some light on a situation of *libertinage* which seems to be already prevalent, although generally only the precursors of the movement, like Bodin who had already written his *Heptaplomeres*, are reckoned with in this period. *Libertinage* seems to have been more advanced at this time than is commonly supposed.

Charron tells us in his preface that he planned originally to write only the third *vérité*, in the belief that the first two *vérités* did not need to be established. But with time he learned that there were some who denied the first *vérité* (the existence of God) and saw in the second (there is a revealed religion and Christ is its founder) a lie and an imposture.[4] Therefore, if it is true that Charron develops the third *vérité* much more than the first two and that it represents the body of the work, it would nevertheless be wrong to dismiss the other two *vérités* as unimportant; Charron himself stressed that the two first *vérités* needed to be firmly established as atheism was already rampant; furthermore, they were the necessary postulated base for proving the Catholic Church to be the only true Church among the Christian faiths.

To dismiss the *trois vérités*, or even the first *vérité*, as unimportant or irrevelant to the study of Charron's philosophy will also prevent a critic from understanding the *Sagesse* which was to follow.

---

[3] Supra, p. 23.

[4] Infra, p. 88.

His detractors have often reproached Charron, a priest, for basing so much of the desired philosophic training of the *sage* on nature and natural law, but a true and serious study of the first *vérité*, which is demonstrated through the use of natural theology, will explain this insistence on natural law found in the *Sagesse*: the *sage*, living according to natural law, will reach through natural theology the first *vérité*, and subsequently the second and the third.

We have said that Charron also felt that it was important to treat the first two *vérités*, for they were already under criticism and attack. He tells us himself[5] that his experience as a priest has proved to him that many so-called Christians do not believe that God exists; they make fun of any "revealed religion", and they do so privately in the presence of tolerant friends whom they want to impress by showing an intellectual outlook which places them above other men.[6]

Charron, with his usual love for classification, sees two kinds of atheists. In the first class he places the few who where born with a predisposition to atheism, and in the second those who have had some religion but who have become indifferent because of the endless religious wars and passionate discussions between the Catholics and the Protestants: "L'apostasie, l'athéisme et l'irreligion sont les reliefs des hérésies."[7]

Reading through the *Mémoires-Journeaux* of Pierre de l'Estoile, we see irreligion and atheism mentioned here and there with the usual outspoken frankness of the author.[8] He names among others a Nicolas, secretary of the King, who was "un bon corrompu et vieil peccheur, et lequel on disait croire en Dieu par bénefice d'inventaire, n'en estant que mieux venu aux compagnies, selon l'humeur corrompue de ce siècle misérable".[9]

Although many critics do not think too highly of Charron's proof of the necessity of religion,[10] I think, on the contrary, that we should note in his method a departure from the scholastic method which

---

[5] Charron, *Vérités*, p. 3.

[6] Garasse must not have read this or he would not have called our *théologal* the "partiarche des esprits forts". This statement also allows us to believe that Charron would never have been on the side of Theophile and of the *libertins*.

[7] *Ibid.*, p. 2.

[8] Pierre de l'Estoile, *Mémoires-Journaux*, Paris: Librairie des Bibliophiles, 1880.

[9] *Ibid.*, vol. VIII, p. 120.

[10] Bonnefon, *op. cit.*, p. 255.

had so long been prevalent, and should admire the neatness of a clear rational proof starting from the most simple considerations and building itself up solidly to the desired conclusion.

First, religion is necessary and good for the "Republic", because it contributed to the establishment and preservation of a community among men. Then, after disserting on the moral value of religion, our *théologal* develops the supernatural phases of his proof and comes to a final argument which, if not formulated with quite as much elegance, is basically the "Pari de Pascal".

Atheism can find place only in a strong and courageous soul since it takes as much character to reject God as it does to find Him and believe in Him. It might take even *more* character, since it is not the easiest path! After a last enumeration of proofs, Charron concludes that there *is* an advantage in believing in God and in his Providence; if you happen to be right, you will have everything to win; if you are not, you won't be any worse than the nonbelievers.[11]

Once Charron's reader has accepted the existence of God and of a natural religion in nature and a natural order which are the expression of God's will, he then will be led to the understanding of revelation and then to a religion revealed by God. Finally, he will come to the acceptance of the Christian Church founded by the Son of God.

This second *vérité* did not present too much difficulty to our *théologal,* and since Protestants and Catholics alike accepted it with equal good will, it didn't warrant lengthy development. This part of the treatise was not really directed against the Moslems, Buddhists, and "autres mécréants" as our preacher called them at the time. The only persons in France for whose benefit this second *vérité* could have been written, were those who laughed at the Churches and the moral obligations Churches imposed upon their members. This attitude was the direct consequence of the denial of the existence of God.[12] It follows that if ever scoffers accepted the first *vérité,* the second *vérité* would become readily acceptable to them as a necessary consequence.

Charron's powerful oratorical talent is displayed quite effectively here when he develops the teaching of Christ and the excellency of the Christian morals. On the solid basis of natural religion our

---

[11] Charron, *Vérités,* p. 98.

[12] Charron, *Vérités,* p. 3.

canon has built with able eloquence the revealed religion of the Son of God.

In his treatment of the first two *vérités* our canon had not done anything new. As we have seen, many Latin treatises had been devoted to the same subject during the long development of the Christian Church, and the man whose *Traité de l'Eglise* Charron combatted principally in his third *vérité*, Duplessis-Mornay, had also written a treatise,[13] *De la vérité de la Religion Chrestienne*, which encompassed the same field as that covered by the first two *vérités*. Our author says this treatise is worth reading and even recommends it.

He also recognizes that the *Traité de l'Eglise* is written "dans un beau style" but is full of errors; the purpose of the third *vérité* is to expose these errors and prove that among so many "créances et opinions qui se disent chrestiennes, la catholique romaine est la seule vraye".[14]

Charron was well prepared for this task, and in reading the *Trois Vérités* we see printed in the margin his sources and the authors he had read. To mention a few, he had read the *Traité de l'Eglise* (which he was trying to refute), Luther, Calvin, Theodore de Bèze and other Protestant theologians. He was as well informed on the Catholic apologists and often cites Bellarmin, Hosius, Cheffonds, Canisius, Florimond and others.

The *Traité de l'Eglise* contains essentially all the substance of Protestantism. To refute it was therefore quite a task, and Charron's long labor extends over some seven hundred pages in which he discusses all the attacks and criticisms made against the Catholic Church. Each time the occation is offered, he shows how the Protestant errors contradict one another. For instance in the same city "ils ont leurs temples séparez" and some Lutherans in Antwerp pretend that "la lythurgie ou Cène des Calvinistes mène une infinité d'âmes à la damnation éternelle".[15]

We also remember that our canon was the proud owner of Ochino's *Catechisme* banned in Zurich and Basel.[16] In his third *vérité* the system Charron uses is really the syllogism. He tells us:

---

[13] Duplessis-Mornay, *De la Vérité de la Religion Chrestienne contre les Athées, Epicuriens, Payens, Juifs, Mahumétans et autres infidèles*, Anvers: 1581.

[14] Duplessis-Mornay, *Traité de l'Eglise*, supra, p. 23.

[15] Charron, *Vérités*, p. 492.

[16] Supra, p. 70.

> C'est dequoy nous sommes en queste en ce livret, duquel la substance et méthode sera telle, réduicte en ce syllogisme, la vraye, certaine et souveraine reigle de nos consciences et juge de la doctrine chrestienne est non l'inspiration privée du Sainct-Esprit, ni l'escriture seule, mais l'Eglise à qui appartient pour nostre regard, omologuer, interpreter et décider des autres deux, inspiration et escriture.[17]

And the Church cannot be wrong in matters of dogma and faith.

Five chapters are devoted to the infallibility and inalienable right of the Church in matters of interpretation. The rest contain the proof that the Roman Church is the only one that keeps the truth pure among the Christian religions. It does this through the authority conferred upon it by tradition, the Church fathers, the infallibility of the councils, and through the primacy of the Holy See in the visible, apostolic, Roman Church.

The author of the *Trois Vérités* had the foresight to limit his discussion to the question of which was the true Church, a problem that Duplessis-Mornay had himself formulated in his *Traité de l'Eglise*. But Duplessis-Mornay had also gone into a number of points of detail which the Reform movement had criticized and found reprehensible in the Catholic Church, and our canon refuses to follow him in this. In his preface Charron had warned us that he would not go into the thousands of little controversies which do nothing but cloud the issue. His purpose is not to refute Duplessis-Mornay point by point but to reach to the heart of the controversy itself. After showing the need for an authority which judges as sovereign judge, our canon points out that the Church came before the Scripture and that free self-interpretation will lead automatically to divisions and subdivisions as already exemplified by the always increasing number of new divergent religious groups in the Reformed Church.

The timing of the publication was also very good since Henry IV was officially converted to the Catholic Church at this time. Catholicism was the traditional faith of the French Kings and of the French people, and Charron, who had used tradition all along as a main argument, insists very cleverly on the matter of traditional faith.

---

[17] Charron, *Vérités*, p. 29.

The Protestant answer was not long in coming[18] and our apologist immediately prepared a second edition of his work,[19] adding to each chapter an "Advertissement et bref examen du premier chapitre de la response faicte au chapitre précédent".

Charron again was answered, and it was then, I believe, after having planned a third edition, that he changed his mind and began work in his *Sagesse*. When we discussed the early criticism[20] of Charron we pointed out that it consisted mainly of answers to the third *vérité* by Protestant pastors or pamphleteers. The tone of these answers, as we have seen, was passionate, with little kindness or reserve. As a matter of fact they are quite in contrast with Charron's manner of criticising Protestant writings. Our canon had always kept a dispassionate and intellectual tone in his discussions and had even praised his opponents whenever their teaching was in accordance with the teaching of the Catholic Church. The numerous additions to the third *vérité* in the 1597 edition of the *Trois Vérités* attempted to keep the discussion in a calm vein, but to no avail, as Gardesy's bellicose pamphlet of 1597 proves to us.[21]

As we know, Charron was already planning a third edition as new pamphlets critical of his *Trois Vérités* were being constantly brought to his attention. His dealings with the League at the time of his stay in Angers in 1589,[22] had taught him how fruitless rational discussion might become when man is deeply convinced of the righteousness of his cause and of the wrongness of the opposition's. It was evident that the *Trois Vérités* had reached an impasse, and any further effort had to be based on something other than the teaching of the Catholic Church, as this teaching was automatically considered by his Protestant adversaries to be perverted because of its very origin. A common basis had to be found from which both Protestants and Catholics could make a fresh start, and it is not by simple coincidence that this is exactly the time that the *Sagesse* started to take shape in Charron's mind. In one of the few surviving letters of Charron to his friend La Rochemaillet, dated March 18, 1597, Charron tells his friend:

[18] Supra, p. 77.

[19] Pierre Charron, *Les Trois Véritéz, seconde édition avec un advertissemènt et bref examen sur la response faicte à la Troisième Vérité, de nouveau imprimée à La Rochelle*, 2d ed., Bourdeaux: Millanges, 1595.

[20] Supra, pp. 23 ff.

[21] Supra, pp. 23 f.

[22] Supra, pp. 75 ff.

> Je me suis mis depuis peu à travailler à mon livre, que je compose avec plaisir. Je me persuade qu'il plaira à certain humeur de gens. Il s'appellera *La Sagesse*. Y aura trois livres. Le premier sera tout achevé avant Pasques et le second avant la Pentecoste.[23]

It took Charron much longer than he calculated, as the first edition of the *Sagesse* did not come off the Millanges press until 1601, but I believe that we can see in this enthusiastic forecast an author excited about a new project he has just conceived and which he is attempting to put into concrete form.

It is probable that he already had written La Rochemaillet about it at least once, because of the wording of the first phrase "Je me suis mis depuis peu à travailler à mon livre...", but the extant letters are few and far apart, and this is the first mention we find of the *Sagesse*.

However in Charron's *Petit Traicté de Sagesse*, which we will study in detail later, we find a passage which shows indubitably that Charron thought of his *Sagesse* as a base for his *Trois Vérités*. He proposes the following as a good plan for the conversion of the Chinese for example: they ought to be taught that worldly knowledge is only vanity and dupery, that humanity is impregnated and torn by capricious opinions it has forged by its own means, that God created man so he will find truth, but that he cannot find it alone or by any human means, and that God himself, who is Truth, should provoke that desire in man and give it to him through revelation. But to be prepared for this revelation man has to rid himself beforehand of all opinions and beliefs, which otherwise would entice him towards some slanted opinion, and then man may very humbly submit to his creator a bare and immaculate soul.[24]

---

[23] Auvray, *op. cit.*, p. 318.

[24] Pierre Charron, *Petit Traicté de Sagesse*, Paris: Feugé, 1642, dernière edition, p. 47. (Sainte-Beuve and Bonnefon, quoting Sainte-Beuve, have partially quoted the same passage to show that Charron was "Chrétien par raison et même orthodoxe, mais päien d'imagination et sceptique par nature d'esprit", Bonnefon, op. cit., pp. 257 f.). "...Que tout savoir du monde n'est que vanité et mensonge, que le monde est congis, déchiré et vilenné, d'opinions fantasques forgées en son serveau. Que Dieu a bien créé l'homme pour cognoistre la vérité, mais qu'il ne la peut cognoistre de soy, ny par aucun moyen humain, et faut que Dieu mesme, au sein duquel elle réside et qui en fait venir l'envie à l'homme, la révèle comme il l'a fait: mais que pour se préparer à cette révelation et lui en faire place, il faut auparavant

L'OCTAVE
CONTENANT
HVICT DISCOVRS
du S. Sacrement.

Auec vn autre discours de la communion des Saincts.

Par M. PIERRE CHARRON Parisien.

A BOVRDEAVS.

Par S. MILLANGES Imprimeur ordinaire du Roy.

1600.
Auec priuilege du Roy.

DISCOVRS
CHRESTIENS

De M. PIERRE CHARRON *Parisien, Chantre & Chanoine, Theologal de l'Eglise Cathedrale de Condom.*

SECONDE PARTIE.

A BOVRDEAVS,

Par SIMON MILLANGES Imprimeur ordinaire du Roy.

1601.
Auec priuilege.

It is true Charron says "for the conversion of the Chinese, for example", but after the impasse to which the direct frontal attack on the third *vérité* had taken him it would have been very poor strategy on his part to propose this plan "for the conversion of Protestants, for example".

Charron had guessed right: the proof that the philosophy offered by the *Sagesse* was found attractive by the Protestants is the success which the *Sagesse* had in England in the seventeenth and eighteenth centuries where we find at least two different translations of the *Sagesse*;[25] the second of these had three different editions. La Rochemaillet tells us that Charron had ready when he died a new edition of the *Trois Vérités* "revues et de beaucoup amplifiez"[26] which the Sieur de Camain, executor of his will, was supposed to publish at his earliest convenience, but unhappily never did. This last information should corroborate our theory that the hope of our canon must have been that his *Sagesse* might provide the *Trois Vérités* with a basis judged acceptable by the adamant Protestant theologians opposing him.

While preparing his *Sagesse* our canon began publishing his *Discours Chrestiens*. The first of these discourses to go to press were *L'Octave contenant huict discours du S. Sacrement, avec un autre discours de la communion des Saints.*[27] In letters[28] to La Rochemaillet written from Condom between October, 1602, and October, 1603, our author often talks about his *Discours de la Divinité*. The last of these was his favorite and he kept adding to it until it was almost a treatise in itself. These many diverse comments by Charron make it difficult to define exactly the nature of the *Discours Chrestiens* which some critics supposed to be sermons he had delivered from the pulpit.

The *Divinité* was written and finished in 1602 for the express purpose of publication under the protection of the bishop of Boulogne. We know this from the letters to La Rochemaillet. Therefore,

---

renoncer et chasser toutes opinions et créances, dont l'esprit est déja anticipé et abbreuvé et le luy présenter nud et blanc et le soubmettre à luy très humblement".

25 Sampson, *Pierre Charron's Of Wisdom*, 1658; George Stanhope, *Pierrė Charron's Of Wisdom*, 1729, 3d ed.

26 *Sagesse*, 1607, *Eloge*, P. XV.

27 Pierre Charron, *L'Octave contenant huict discours du S. Sacrement, avec un autre discours de la communion des Saints*, Bourdeaux: Millanges, 1600.

28 Auvray, *op. cit.*, pp. 323 ff.

DISCOVRS CHRESTIEN,

QV'IL N'EST PERMIS NY LOISIBLE A VN SVBIECT, pour quelque cause & raison que ce soit, de se Liguer, bander, & rebeller contre son Roy

Par P. C. P. Chantre & Chanoine Theologal de Condom.

A PARIS,
Chez DAVID LE CLERC, ruë Frementel, au Petit Corbeil.
M. D. CVI.
Avec Permission.

DISCOVRS CHRESTIEN,

SVR LA BENEDICTION DONNEE PAR ISAAC A IACOB son fils puisné, pensant la donner à Esau son aisné.

Par P. Charron Parisien Chantre & Chanoine Theologal en l'Eglise de Condom.

A PARIS,
Par DAVID LE CLERC, ruë Frementel, au Petit Corbeil.
M. D. CVI.
Avec Permission.

DISCOVRS CHRESTIENS DE LA DIVINITE CREATION REDEMTION ET OCTAVES DV Sainct Sacrement.

PAR M. PIERRE CHARron Parisien, Docteur Theologal, Chanoine en l'Eglise de Condon.

A PARIS.
Chez ROBERT BERTAVLT Marchand Libraire au mont St Hilaire a l'estoille couronnee.
M. DCXXII.

most of the *Divinité* was not delivered in sermon form. The same is true of the *Création,* since it is almost a treatise on physics. Charron writes himself: "Toute la physique y est entrée, mais à ma mode."[29]

On the other hand we have his *Discours Chrestien sur la bénédiction donnée par Isaac à Jacob son fils puisné pensant la donner à Esaü son aisné.* It was published by La Rochemaillet in 1606 with the *Petit Traicté de Sagesse* and the *Discours qu'il n'est permis ny loisible à un subject pour quelque cause et raison que ce soit, de se liguer, bander et rebeller contre son Roy.*[30]

In a letter to La Rochemaillet,[31] on the tenth of March 1603, Charron said that the *Bénédiction de Jacob* (referring to the abovementioned discourse) does not deserve to be printed since it is "un petit avorton". We know from its subtitle that it was a sermon delivered in the presence of Marguerite de France, Reine de Navarre.

We can therefore assume that he kept his sermons, and that he intended to publish some of them in groups that would be related to each other, and would compose additional discourses to fill in or complete some collections and help the general cohesiveness of the work.

I believe this is why Charron's biographers have always been vague about the *Discours Chrestiens* and merely mention them as the published sermons of a preacher. Sabrié is the only one to write at length on the *Discours Chrestiens.* He uses them to show Charron's talent as a preacher and the great inspiration he showed in speaking of the sacraments which were at this time under the fire of the Protestants.[32] Charron considers, for instance, the bread and the wine ennobled when it becomes the Divinity at consecration, and he invites his readers to follow the example of the humble bread and wine and cast off their human limitations to join themselves intimately with God.

Being a humanist, he finds subjects for comparison in pagan antiquity and uses them with far-reaching effect. He asks the Christians to be as united in the partaking of the body and blood

---

[29] *Ibid.,* p. 328.

[30] Pierre Charron, *Traicté de Sagesse, plus quelques discours Chrestiens,* Paris: Le Clerc, 1606.

[31] Auvray, *op. cit.,* p. 325.

[32] Sabrié, *op. cit.,* p. 181.

of Christ as Catiline's conspirators were by the drinking of a mixture of their own blood as a sign of unshakable trust in each other.

Sabrié concludes that Charron more than once must have reached the summit of eloquence. The doctrine he presents has firmness and vigor, his thought is powerful but concise, and his high and noble conception of the faith is developed with proper austerity. And Charron is excellent as long as he wrote as a *prédicateur-théologien,* but at times he may have become too theological.[33]

Moreover, La Rochemaillet tells us of our preacher's concept of the three ways to "discourir et déclarer en public ses conceptions".[34] In laying down these precepts, Charron denounces the methods used by the Sorbonne to teach, train, and evaluate.

The first way to preach or discourse is to follow the accepted rules and the precepts of the art of sermonizing: etymologizing, distinguishing between the name and the matter, defining, dividing, subdividing, and studying causes, effects, and accidents. This method is fitted only for schools and the instruction of apprentices.

The second is to collect the opinions and sayings of others with citations of places, books and chapters; this method was in use among the doctors and the preachers. Such sermons are, however, seldom more than long enumerations of commonplaces compiled by people who, having little or nothing to say of their own, let others speak for them. Too often though, they add to his proof of ignorance and weakness by quoting and interpreting in a fashion contrary to common sense. They esteem it scholarly to quote a great deal, forgetting that quotations, necessary as they are for controversies to be decided and positions to be defended by authority, should at least be pertinent, well chosen, and persuasive. This method, which is obviously the Sorbonne's way of argumentation, was considered by Charron, says La Rochemaillet, as the least effective of the three.

The third method, which Charron preferred, contained the essence of the first two without seeming to do so and without being subject to the order and regulations of the art. In the light of Charron's writing and of the training he recommended for the *sage,* I would understand that in his preaching Charron used formal logic and rhetoric only in the measure that it lent clarity to his sermons, defining the points he wanted to treat and the exact meaning of

---

[33] Sabrié, *op. cit.,* p. 188.

[34] Charron, *Sagesse,* 1607, *Eloge,* p. XIII.

DE LA SAGESSE

LIVRES TROIS.

Par M. PIERRE LE CHARRON,

Parisien, Chanoine Theologal & Chantre en l'Eglise Cathedrale de Comdom.

A BOVRDEAVS,

Par SIMON MILLANGES Imprimeur ordinaire du Roy. 1601.

Avec privilege.

certain keywords he used. Similarly quotations and general opinions are used only after they have been fairly well assimilated by the author and only sparingly so to lend authority to reasoning and thought and not to represent the body of the sermon. Used in the most celebrated homilies of the past and held in honor in antiquity, this brand of eloquence is more noble. Judgment, understanding and imagination are its chief qualities, whereas the other brands of eloquence rely essentially on memory. Furthermore, this third method is more pleasing and profitable to listeners and students, since it is directed rather toward judgment than toward learning. It will tend to strengthen judgment and conscience rather than to fill the memory with meaningless quotations and names as the first two methods do.

All but two of Pierre Charron's *Discours Chrestiens*[35] were published posthumously by his friend La Rochemaillet in 1604. The *Discours* previously published in 1600 and 1601 in Bordeaux were published again at this time. Two discourses which were found later were published with the *Petit Traicté de Sagesse*;[36] and all of them were published again in 1635 in *Toutes les Oeuvres de Pierre Charron.*[37]

On the fourth of June, 1598, Charron who was at the time a canon at Cahors, wrote his friend La Rochemaillet that two-thirds of his *Sagesse* was completed and that he hoped to complete it by fall.[38] But we find later through another letter that it was not finished until April, 1599.

Finally in 1601 the first edition of the *Sagesse*[39] came off of the Millanges press. The delay was probably due to the securing of the *privilège*. With the publication of the *Sagesse* our preacher-theologian had attained the rank of philosopher.

La Sagesse is divided into three parts in order to connect it structurally with *Les Trois Vérités*. Charron tells us in his preface that his purpose in the first book is to teach man to know himself through a thorough self-examination. The second book teaches him through general advice and discipline to control his behavior and

---

[35] Pierre Charron, *Discours Chrestiens de la Divinité, Création, Rédemption et Octave du Saint-Sacrement,* Paris: Berthault, 1604.

[36] Supra, p. 97.

[37] Pierre Charron, *Les Oeuvres Complètes de Pierre Charron,* Paris: Jacques Villery, 1635.

[38] Auvray, *op. cit.,* p. 319.

[39] Pierre Le Charron, *De la Sagesse,* Bourdeaux: Millanges, 1601.

to be moderate in all things. In the third book, this instruction is completed by the teaching of the four moral virtues "Prudence, Justice, Strength, Temperance", which should govern the lives of men through a sense of duty and honesty. He concludes by telling us:

> Voilà pourquoi cette oeuvre, qui instruit la vie et les moeurs à bien vivre et à bien mourir, est intitulée *Sagesse*, comme la nôtre précédente qui instruisait à bien croire a été appelée *Vérité* ou bien *Les Trois Vérités* y ayant trois livres en celle-ci comme en celle-là.[40]

Charron wants to teach man "à bien vivre et à bien mourir". In his preface he defines his *Sagesse* as being:

> ...preu de prudence, c'est à dire preud'homie avec habilité, probité bien advisée... Preud'hommie sans prudence est sotte et indiscrette; prudence sans preud'homie n'est que finesse: ce sont les deux choses les meilleures et plus excellentes, et les chefs de tout bien; mais seules et séparées sont défaillantes et imparfaictes. *La Sagesse* les accouple.

This is what Charron means by *Sagesse*: the alliance of experienced probity and integrity with discreet prudence. He insists again and again on the two characteristics of his *Sagesse* which were so lacking in many of his contemporaries: "Bien se connaître, constamment être bien réglé, modéré en toutes choses, par toutes choses."

One of the best ways to study the *Sagesse* and to understand the intentions of its author is to start with the *Traicté de Sagesse* or *Petit Traicté de Sagesse*,[41] the last work of our canon. The critics of Charron have always neglected the *Traicté*, dismissing it as a "sommaire de son livre, et une apologie et réponse aux plaintes et objections qu'on faisait contre icelui".[42] This however is where special interest[43] of the *Traicté de Sagesse* lies, and it is for the *Sagesse* what the *Examens* are for Corneille's plays, that is to say,

---

[40] Pierre Charron, *Sagesse*, 1607, Preface of 1601 ed., Reprinted, p. 745.

[41] The edition used here is: Pierre Charron, *Traicté de Sagesse*, Paris: Robert Feugé, 1642, dernière êdition.

[42] Bonnefon, *op. cit.*, p. 307.

[43] J. D. Charron, *op. cit.*, p. 121.

TRAICTE DE SAGESSE COMPOSE' PAR Pierre Charron Parisien Docteur és Droicts, Chantre & Chanoine Theologal de Condom.

PLVS QVELQVES DISCOVRS Chrestiens du mesme Aucteur, qui ont esté trouvez apres son decez, avec son portraict au naturel, & l'Eloge ou sommaire de sa vie.

Le tout dedié à Monseigneur de HARLAY premier President.

A PARIS, Par DAVID LE CLERC, ruë Frementel au Petit Corbeil.

M. D C V I.

Avec Privilege du Roy.

TRAICTE DE SAGESSE COMPOSE PAR PIERRE CHARRON parisien, Docteur és Droicts, Chantre & Chanoine Theologal de Cõdom.

PLVS QVELQVES DISCOVRS Chrestiens du mesme Autheur, qui ont esté trouvez, apres son decez, avec son portraict au naturel, & l'Eloge ou sommaire de sa vie.

Le tout dedié à Monseigneur de HARLAY premier President.

A PARIS, Par DAVID LE CLERC, ruë Frementel au petit Corbeil, prés le puits Certain.

M. D. C. VIII.

Avec Privilege du Roy.

TRAICTE DE SAGESSE COMPOSE' PAR PIERRE CHARRON parisien, Docteur es droicts, Chantre & Chanoine Theologal de Condom.

PLVS QVELQVES DISCOVRS Chrestiens du mesme Autheur, qui ont esté trouvez apres son decez, avec son pourtraict au naturel.

Le tout dedié à Monseigneur de HARLAY premier President.

TROISIESME EDITION.

A PARIS, Chez MARTIN DVRAND, ruë sainct Iacques, à l'enseigne du Roy David.

M. D. C. XIIII.

Avec Privilege du Roy.

self-criticism directed mainly towards answering attacks formulated by those criticizing him.

The *Traicté de Sagesse* was published in 1601 and dedicated to Monseigneur Me Achilles de Harlay, *conseiller du Roy,* in accordance with the intention of Pierre Charron. The publication of this was the final work of homage of his faithful and courageous friend, Michel de la Rochemaillet, who worked tirelessly for three years, surmounting all obstacles, to put into print all of the philosopher's remaining compositions. In his dedicatory epistle[44] La Rochemaillet tells us a little about the purpose of this explanatory and polemic pamphlet and why it was written.

Charron wrote the *Traicté* a few months before his death and he meant to make it an abstract of his *De la Sagesse,* a defense answering complaints and objections, a short and general picture of his *Sagesse,* and a declaration of his intended purpose in writing it.

The author of the *De la Sagesse* had foreseen that his book would be poorly received by ordinary people encumbered with superstitions and would be severely censured by the presumptuous who pretend to know everything and consider themselves to be the wisest among men. In a short introductory preface Pierre Charron describes the two kinds of adversaries whom he calls the ignorant, the coarse, and the hypocrites. He reminds us that he did not write for the ordinary people. In his *De la Sagesse* he condemned their common and popular opinions as being usually erroneous. If they had received it with enthusiasm, then his *Sagesse* would have been "bien descheu de ses prétentions". As for the hypocrites, they feign not to understand him well or not to understand him at all. They give other meanings to his statements, or deliberately misinterpret them.

These insincere men of Charron's generation are the precursors of those who throughout the following generations used the *De la Sagesse* to prove their own theses or to discredit our author. According to our philosopher, they attempt to discredit him by perverting what he gave as facts into rights and duties, by interpreting his facts as opinions and by viewing what were only propositions as final decisions. They also impute to him as his own opinion what

---

[44] Pierre Charron, *Traicté de Sagesse,* "Epistre à Monseigneur Me. Achilles de Harlay, chevalier et seigneur de Beaumont, Conseiller du Roy en ses conseils d'Estat et Privé, premier President en sa cour de Parlament", by Gabriel de la Rochemaillet.

belongs to others. Statements he issued as his honest human opinion were immediately made relevant to religion and divine belief; and when he spoke of virtue and morals and natural action, they applied it to Grace and supernatural action. Finally, what was only the fruit of his mind and his personal experience was immediately connected with his profession and his position as a churchman.

It is against these hypocrites that the *Traicté de Sagesse* is directed, and it is in this light that we are going to study it, chapter by chapter.

Chapter 1.—First, Charron gives us a more detailed definition of his *Sagesse*.[45] He attempts to be more precise and to try to substantiate his ideal of *sagesse* with a few concrete examples for the benefit of those who are always ready to misinterpret his thought. He calls it "Qualité suffisante ou habitude non commune, ni populaire, mais excellente, singulière et relevée par dessus le commun et ordinaire, soit en bien ou en mal."[46] This goes a little further than just "preu de prudence, preud'hommie".[47] He therefore asserts that this is the uncommon quality of the good as well as of the bad. He continues by quoting from Latin, "Sapientes sunt ut faciant mala".[48] His *sagesse* is not necessarily a quality good in itself and worthy of praise but "excellente, exquise et singulière en quoy que soit", and could be applied as well to any person, pirate, tyrant, thief, wise king, or captain. By *excellente, exquise et singulière* Pierre Charron means superior, distinguished, and out of the ordinary.

His *sagesse* is control of self through containment and moderation; it is opposed not only to folly and debauchery, but also to lowness and vulgarity, because this *sagesse* implies strength through self-control, distinction, and general superiority of character. Subsequently one could distinguish three types of *sagesse*: Divine, Human, and Worldly; corresponding to God, pure and wholesome nature, and vicious and corrupted nature.

The worldly or mundane *sagesse* (the least worthy of the three *sagesses*) concerns itself only with how to reach a successful and desirable position in society. It manifests itself in several different forms according to the kind of worldliness governing it. These kinds are: wealth, passion, egotism, and ambition; and each in its own way and through excesses can readily lead to a corresponding vice.

[45] Previous definition supra, pp. 100 f.
[46] Charron, *Traicté*, Ch. I.
[47] Supra, p. 101.
[48] Pierre Charron, *Traicté*, p. 3.

I wonder if at this point Charron thought of a contemporary treatise mainly concerned with this worldly *sagesse,* the *De la Sagesse* of Beroalde de Verville, who is mostly known however because of his *Le Moyen de Parvenir.*[49]

The divine *sagesse* is metaphysical and has a double nature. Through the knowledge of divine things one can pass judgment on human actions. Human wisdom is acquired through study and is the field of philosophers; divine *sagesse* is infused, given by God. This divine wisdom is not treated in his *De la Sagesse.* It was the material of the first of his *Trois Vérités* and of his *Discours de la Divinité.*

This treatise is on "human wisdom". Philosophers and theologians define this human wisdom as beautiful and noble straightforwardness existing in a man internally and externally, in his thoughts, words, actions, and movements. It is the "Excellence et perfection de l'homme comme homme", and one has this human *sagesse* if he knows how to act well as a man.

How can this human wisdom be attained? Pierre Charron offers two means. One is what he calls the *conformation originelle,* that is to say, that man should be prepared and educated to receive wisdom, although people do not pay much attention to this means or consider it basic to wisdom. They do not prepare themselves for the procreation of their children. He adds, "...or c'est à quoy l'on pense le moins et à peine pense-t-on tout simplement à faire enfans, mais seulement comme bestes d'assouvir son plaisir..."

The second means is through the study of philosophy and especially the study of natural law, which should guide and rule our lives like a lamp. He tells us "Morale, c'est la vray science de l'homme; tout le reste au pris d'elle n'est que vanité." Ethics will

---

[49] Beroalde de Verville, *De la Sagesse, Livre premier. Auquel il est traicté du Moyen de parvenir au parfaict estat de bien vivre, remédier aux afflictions, embrasser la constance, et trouver l'èntier contentement selon l'institution Divine,* Tours: Janet Mettayer, 1593.

In his *Bibliographie d'Editions Originales* Tchermazine says that this *De la Sagesse* of Beroalde is the main reason why *Le Moyen de Parvenir* has been attributed to him. Beroalde de Verville, *Le Moyen de Parvenir, oeuvre contènant la raison de tout ce qui a esté est et sera: avec démonstrations certaines et nécessaires, selon la rencontre des effets de vertu. Et adviendra que ceux qui auront nez à portèr lunette s'en serviront, ainsi qu'il est escrit au dictionnaire à dormir en toutes langues.* S. imprimé ceste année.

According to Brunet's *Manuel du Libraire* this edition of *Le Moyen de Parvenir* would be the first. No name of places, publisher, or dates are given.

teach us "à bien vivre et bien mourir"; that is the main objective, since it is equivalent to Charron's definition of *sagesse*: "un preu de prudence, une habile et forte preud'hommie, une probité bien advisée".[50]

If you have experienced the first means of *conformation originelle* you will be disposed to wisdom without any trouble, otherwise you should do as Socrates did and correct your defective nature through the study of philosophy.

Chapter 2.—In this chapter Charron develops the famous Socratic phrase γνωθι σεαυτον, 'know thyself'. We should know well the subject which we are treating and also try to make our pupils wise. The proper subject of study is man, and by man Charron means the human condition and particularly one's own human condition. This study is usually very difficult since man hides so much of his true inner self from others and even from himself. It seems that everyone takes pleasure in deceiving himself, "...se flattant et chatoüillant pour se faire rire, atténuant ses défauts, en chérissant ce qu'il a de bon".

Man seems never to examine himself from within, but to be always outside himself, musing, proud of himself, criticizing and advising others, professing knowledge and great virtue but not even aware of his own shortcomings, faults and vices. But: "Seul sage se cognoist, et qui bien se connoist sage est."

And then Charron adds a remark of the kind that made him so popular with the *libertins* of the seventeenth century: the wise man does his duty and keeps the law, not because they are laws but because of respect for himself. He is above the laws and he does not need them; they are for the mass, and even if there were none, the wise man would behave no differently. Using such a passage, a seventeenth-century *libertin* could pretend that, being above the mass by his training, he could disregard the Church laws. However, I do not think that Charron means this; I believe that he refers there to the *morale naturelle,* or conscience. In his definition of *sagesse* and the means of acquiring it, he had advocated the study of ethics of which natural law is a part.[51] He must have had in mind the *morale naturelle* since he says, referring to the freedom of will required for the existence of conscience, "pleine, noble géné-

---

[50] Supra, p. 100, previous definition.
[51] Supra, p. 105.

reuse liberté, par laquelle le sage, quitte et net de tout erreur et passion, considère et juge toutes choses".

After discussing natural law, Charron recommends to the *sage* two attitudes which we are to find later as the first two steps of the *Discours de la Méthode.*

He tells us, "Solum certum nihil esse certi, hoc unum scio quod nihil scio";[52] the only certain thing is that nothing is certain; the only thing I know is that I know nothing. Truth and lies coexist in us and are made valid by identical means. The "Que sais-je?" of Montaigne has become "Je ne sais!"

Then the next step:

> Voir, considérer, éxaminer et juger de toutes choses; rien ne doit éschapper au sage qu'il ne le mette sur le bureau et en la balance... pour juger il se faut despouiller de tout, se mettre à nud, considérer les choses de sang froid, comme proposées tout de nouveau.[53]
>
> ...(ce) qu'il faut joindre au précédent est une surséance et indifférence de jugement par laquelle l'homme considérant tout comme dict est froidement et sans passion, ne s'aheurte ni ne se lie ou oblige à aucune chose mais se tient libre, universel et ouvert à tout, toujours prêt à recevoir la vérité si elle se présente...[54]

It is most interesting to find Charron a remote precursor of the Cartesian method just as we had found him the precursor of the *Pari de Pascal.*[55]

The next quality of the wise man, *prud'hommie,* is the result of the qualities already examined. It will come automatically from the complete knowledge of oneself after doubt has brought one to a careful examination and judgment of all things. "Estre et consentir de vivre homme" is equivalent for the wise man to "Estre et vouloir estre homme de bien".

Again Charron insists on obedience to the Church laws, asserting that because of his complete understanding of the law of con-

---

[52] Charron, *Traicté,* p. 12.
[53] *Ibid.,* p. 16.
[54] *Ibid.,* p. 21.
[55] Supra, p. 89.

science the *sage* will always entirely fulfill his duties to God, himself, and his neighbor. But he will always keep the natural law[56] sovereign, universal and infallible, and believe it and follow it.

Chapter 3.—Another good way to describe a man of wisdom is to paint the man who is the contrary of all that wisdom presupposes. His mind is weak, insipid and always biased and stubbornly inclined toward certain opinions. He is unable to modify or to soften his judgements, and if he has any learning it will make him only more presumptuous, stubborn and rash.

This man is naturally the enemy of wisdom, and Charron tells us that it is particularly against such men that he is making war in his *De la Sagesse.* He designates them by the name of *pédant* because he cannot think of a better term.

Evidently many professors in the arts and sciences thought that they were the *pédants* of the *De la Sagesse.* But our philosopher declares frankly that he does not call any of the "estat de robe longue ou profession littéraire" *pédant.*

Then he opposes again the *sage* to the *pédant.* The former is open-minded and not afraid of the unfamiliar; the latter is narrow-minded, stubborn and rash. The former opposes his joyous, soft, and understanding character to the rashness and harshness of the latter. Modestly, with careful and doubtful words, the wise man says, "Je ne scay, peut-être, il semble", whereas the *pédant* uses authority as a basis.

Chapter 4.—It was very clever of Charron to bring the reader of his treatise to see all the adversaries of the *De la Sagesse* grouped together as people incapable of wisdom. In this chapter he reviews the main criticisms and attacks made on his treatise. Some say that his *sagesse* is new, that he is venturing into a still untrod path and that consequently his propositions are paradoxical and his presentation daring and peculiar. Developing this criticism, Charron observes that the man of wisdom shocks the ordinary man because he is concerned only with goodness and internal and essential values. He thus appears as a paradox, a censor scorning the world. Our canon is well pleased with this criticism and takes it as a compliment.

To those who reproach him for not treating of God and religion, he answers, "Je traicte icy de la sagesse humaine et philosophyquement, et non de la divine théologalement".

---

[56] Natural law and conscience are used identically here.

Some object to his intention to subject everything to re-examination as too dangerous. The doctors of the Sorbonne must have been among these! But Pierre Charron asks them if they know of anything more natural, proper, and worthy for man than to judge—that is, to consider, examine, and weigh all things. If you deprive him of all that, does it not reduce him to an animal status? Man cannot be so vile and frightened that he could not make use of his highest and noblest attribute, his mind.

Then our canon discusses the accusation of Pyrrhonism[57] made against the philosophy of his *De la Sagesse*. He admits that his doctrine has some surface similarity to Pyrrhonism but that there is a great difference between them. He advocates that the man of wisdom adhere to the best and the most probable, and that he be always ready to accept something better when it appears. Let us add that Pyrrho is against any definite decision since to each proposition an equally probable contrary proposition can be opposed; and we have seen that Charron demands that the man of wisdom pass judgment on everything.

The author of the *Sagesse* saved for the end the discussion of the criticism involving the real value of his philosophy. Some would ask if blind obedience to established principles would not be more satisfactory for the soul and the mind than the indecision and suspense involved in questioning everything. Charron answers this in his usual logical fashion by going back again to his definition of the man of wisdom, "Ouy aux fols, non aux sages".

The greatest and most noble philosophers have achieved peace of mind by practising this philosophy. But some people cannot live free. Their minds have to be enslaved to an idea; obstinate and enflamed by their opinion they enjoy condemning all others without reserve. Even if you convince them they will not give up, although sometimes they will change their minds and will turn around and combat their former opinions as stubbornly as ever. These do not know what truth is. They don't even know the meaning of "To know".

As for the "principles", if they do not come from God, the True Principle, they should be examined; it would betray weakness to accept them without question. Theology, like mysticism,[58] teaches

---

[57] The Pyrrhonians are sceptics from the school of Pyrrho (Greek philosopher, 360 B. C.) who doubted or affected to doubt everything and who believed that philosophers should refrain from reaching conclusions.

[58] Science of mystic devotion.

us that to be well prepared for God and his work in us we have to empty and clean our soul, to make it bare and free from all prejudice and belief in order to let God live and act in it. This is already an answer to the attacks on Charron by the Jesuit Garasse[59] in his *Apologie*.

The philosopher-preacher ends this chapter reminding us again that his exhortation to follow natural law does not mean that he believes it to be sufficient. He does not deny God's grace, and if he does not mention it and does not treat the theological virtues, it is because, as he has already told us, his subject is *La sagesse humaine* and not *La sagesse divine*.

Chapter 5.—In this final chapter Pierre Charron acknowledges that a number of criticisms have been expressed. He does not try to refute them; on the contrary, he reaffirms his stand and seems rather pleased that some were shaken by his attitude.

He tells us that anyone who knows humanity and has a strong character will not let himself be shaken by unreasonable objections. He has already condemned chauvinism in all of its forms. One should admit, he says, that among Indians, Chinese, cannibals, Turks, and other nations which are generally considered barbarian, there are often customs and institutions as good as or better than our own. One should be able to admit that many things considered to be miracles, enchantments, works of the devils, etc., are only natural or artificial effects of human imagination. Physical suffering is not the only evil, and death, cuckoldry, sterility, and poverty are not really evil in themselves. It is imperative to open one's mind to new concepts however shocking they may be, in order to be capable of progress. He tells people who do not like his treatise *De la Sagesse* that he wants them to feel free to hold that opinion. After all, he had exhorted them to judge freely of all things. But they do not have to be angry with him, since he certainly won't be angry with them if they do not approve of it.

It is good if some people do not finds some of his statements to their liking. That is partly why he has formulated them; they will force such people to think. If others have any suggestions he is ready to listen, but asks them to omit the scholastic viewpoint since it is valid only in matters of religion.[60]

---

[59] Garassse, *Apologie*, Paris: 1624.

[60] He pays respect here to the Sorbonne.

In ending his pamphlet Pierre Charron invites his readers to practice good sense and to refrain from judging or condemning those who differ from them in action and opinion. As for himself, he urges obedience to superiors and to laws, probity, virtue, and the reform of passions and vices, and he feels that his *De la Sagesse* will accomplish much towards that goal.

In conclusion we could apply to the eloquent treatise *De la Sagesse* what its author himself had said of eloquence in the last sentence of his work. The *Sagesse* has been misused, misunderstood: "This is true but for this very reason the *Sagesse* should not receive scorn, as it shares with the best things in this world the faculty of being diverted for good or bad according to the disposition of those who control them; most men have misused their brains, but that does not mean that one shouldn't have any".[61]

---

[61] Charron, *Sagesse*, 1607, p. 744, "Cela est vray et pour cela n'est-elle pas à mespriser, cela luy est commun avec toutes les plus excellentes choses du monde, de pouvoir estre tournée à mal et à bien, selon que celui qui les possede est mal disposé; la plus part des hommes abusent de leur entendement, ce n'est à dire qu'il n'en faille avoir".

CHAPTER VI

TOWARDS A NEW CHARRON

As the fever generated by the wars of religion was abating under the calming influence and the efficient government of the *bon roy Henry*, the rising dangers of atheism seen by Charron to be the direct result of the religious strife[1] became more and more evident.

As we have seen, our canon in the preface of his *Trois Vérités* expresses the thought that few were born with godless tendencies and that most of the unbelievers had reached that state of mind because of the endless religious wars and passionate discussions between the Catholics and the Protestants.[2] To a person of weak religious principle, the crimes committed in the name of religion by both Catholics and Protestants were a great deterrent to piety. Well aware of this, precisely in his chapter on piety,[3] Charron exclaims:

> Tantum religio potuit suadere malorum...
> Quae peperit scelerosa atque impia facta.[4]

Zealousness in religion has caused so many ignominious villainies that there are some who think that the least they can do is to hate those who have other religious opinions and avoid them as one would the pestilence. A few will choose to kill a fellowman for this

[1] Supra, p. 88.

[2] Supra, pp. 88 f.

[3] Charron, *Sagesse*, 1604, p. 379.

[4] *Ibid.*, p. 400, "...How could religion suggest so many crimes... so many scoundrel and impious actions have been perpetrated in its name". Lucretius, vol. I, lines 102 and 83.

very same reason and will believe their action in doing so well received by the Lord.

Omnis qui interficiet vos,
putabit se obsequium praestare Deo.[5]

Charron's condemnation of religious intolerance is categorical, and he sees as a lack of human wisdom and good sense the pretense of one's belief that betrayal, rebellion, and all kind of crimes will be permissible and commendable if they are committed for the betterment and progress of religion.

Charron was also aware of the responsibilities of the princes. He writes of this matter in the chapter entitled "Devoir des Souverains et Sujets"[6] insisting that the prince should not only fear God but should also care for the preservation of religion in his state, and keep inviolate both the laws of God and of nature as well as his promises and agreements "avec ses sujets ou autres y ayans interest".

When writing these lines the author of the *Sagesse* probably had in mind the publication of the decrees of the Council of Trent in France which would have cleared away so many evils then afflicting the Gallican Church by eliminating many abuses perpetrated by the civil power upon the spiritual.[7]

When examining the progress of irreligion, one notes that in the early years of the seventeenth century its physical causes, the religious wars, were fading quickly into the past like a gladly forgotten plague while the intellectual causes were beginning to be placed under scrutiny.

If some authors were placed in a class by themselves because of their intellectual outlook, as were Bodin or Du Vair, others like Montaigne and Charron were placed together because of apparently similar attitudes towards scepticism, stoicism and the concept of human wisdom.

To this we should add the fact that they were both much read and discussed and were *ipso facto* the link between humanism and rationalism in France: there I believe is the beginning of the traditional concept of the Montaigne-Charron intellectual affiliation.

---

[5] *Ibid.*, p. 400.
[6] Charron, *Sagesse*, 1607, p. 662.
[7] Supra, Ch. III.

Montaigne had said:

> On couche volontiers le sens des escris d'autrui à la faveur des opinions qu'on a prejugées en soi: et un atheiste se flatte à ramener tous autheurs à l'atheisme: infectant de son propre venin la matière innocente.[8]

This was true not only for him, but even more so for Charron, since they were becoming unwilling participants in the fight of the Garasses and Mersennes against the *libertins.*[9] Because of their essence, however, the *Essays* were partially exonerated and the *Sagesse* remained the main subject of suspicion.

In summarising the opinions of contemporary critics,[10] Sorel, in an attempt at unbiased criticism, had reported the judgments of Charron's detractors and how he had been called the "secrétaire de Montaigne" and his "petit disciple". This was to become the cliché in the criticism concerned with our canon, "Charron, disciple de Montaigne".

If these are the facts, it would be interesting to try to explain why these critics reacted as they did. However, we will limit ourselves here to the point which we believe should be solved first: the degree of intellectual affiliation between Montaigne and Charron. At the same time it will follow that changing that concept will make necessary a complete re-evaluation of the opinion in which Charron's philosophy is held in modern criticism.

After the first few years of the turn of the century, we find no further attacks on Charron emanating from identifiable Protestant sources. This might be explained by the fact that Protestant rights had been protected by the Edict of Nantes and they no longer felt the same compulsion to defend their doctrine in pamphlets that they had felt earlier. In the following decades, the discussions about Charron are carried on by the following three groups: the Sorbonneurs, last-ditch defenders of scholasticism who had been so plainly exposed and condemned in the *Sagesse* and *Petit Traicté de Sagesse*; the intellectual *libertins*, or shall we say the *raisonneurs*, who find the *Sagesse* a tool for their intellectual achievements; and their opponents, the Catholic polemists who try to oppose the fast-growing

---

[8] Montaigne, *Les Essais*, Villey edition, Paris: Alcan, 1922, vol. 2, XII, p. 159.

[9] Supra, p. 27.

[10] Supra, p. 32.

rationalism they deem dangerous to the faith.[11] The last two groups are the most important ones since the main action of the Sorbonne was to try to prohibit the printing of the *Sagesse*, and to condemn "les idées dangereuses comme trop advancées" of its author.[12]

To Gassendi and Naudé, for instance, the *Sagesse* was an excellent treatise; in fact, they considered it superior to the *Essays* of Montaigne. This was to infuriate Sainte-Beuve who failed to understand that they did so because of an intellectual, rather than a literary point of view. Furthermore, we ought to say that the *Sagesse* is quite equal to—if not superior to the *Essays* from a "moral" point of view—for any generation of critics. The *Sagesse* was more suited to the purpose of the *libertins* because of its very detailed and precise plan, in which propositions and discussions followed each other clearly and in carefully arranged sequence.

The adversaries of *libertinage* employed a double tactic in knocking the preacher-philosopher from the pedestal where the *libertins* had placed him: first they tried to ruin his reputation as a churchman and as a writer and, secondly, they tried to show that he was "a little disciple and imitator" of a man who espoused the same type of moral philosophy, Montaigne. This tactic, worthless as far as the Naudés and Gassendis were concerned, was effective with the average seventeenth-century Frenchman who was influenced more by literary than by rational aspirations and was more apt to enjoy the *Essays* than the *Sagesse*.

An unbiased literary critic, like Sorel, could only mention briefly the divergent critical tendencies and attempt to stand safely between them, rejecting what was most extreme on both sides in an effort to reconcile them.

When the criticism of Charron was revived in the nineteenth century by Sainte-Beuve,[13] the point of view of the author of the *Lundis* was self-explanatory; he could not understand how, as we have just explained it, some "bons esprits, médiocres juges en cela" had found Charron equal or superior to Montaigne.

Sainte-Beuve's judgment of Charron was welcomed by the Faguets and Lansons, for they endeavored, with their love for classification, to see one author as the star of a period and all others as planets or satellites revolving in well-defined orbits about him.[14]

---

[11] Supra, Ch. II.

[12] Charron, *Sagesse*, 1607, *Eloge*.

[13] Supra, p. 38.

[14] Supra, p. 41.

Their disciples have respected their views and, although some definite progress and discoveries were made in the study of the author of the *Sagesse* by Bonnefon and Sabrié, the true place and merits of Charron have never been recognised. However, he is not the only author to suffer such a fate; only during recent years, many other so-called second or third-rank authors have been restored to a more deserved position; among them Agrippa d'Aubigné and Du Bartas, to name only two from the same period as our author.[15]

Although Sabrié still considers Charron *l'Herbier de Montaigne,*[16] this critic has seen and shown Charron's influence on men as important in the history of the philosophic movement in France as Saint-Evremond and Jean Jacques Rousseau.

After showing that Saint-Evremond, although a great admirer of the *Essays,* had nevertheless paralleled closely in his philosophical outlook the system of morality of the author of the *Sagesse,*[17] Sabrié proved the great influence of our canon on the author of the *Emile.*[18]

We have shown that Rousseau had had in his hands at least two different editions of the *Sagesse.*[19] We have the testimony of the Marquis de Luchet to this effect.[20] But Rousseau mentioned our *théologal* only once in order to identify the profession of faith of his *Vicaire* Savoyard by comparing it to a declaration of faith Pierre Charron could have professed.[21]

According to Sabrié, the fundamentals of the *Discours sur les Sciences et les Arts* and *Discours sur l'origine de l'inégalité parmi les hommes* can be found in condensed forms in some paragraphs of the *Sagesse.*[22] In the *Emile* Rousseau agrees throughout with Charron's ideas on how to care for a child after his birth and how to train him during the early formative years. Charron's influence was felt long after his time, and he was appreciated for his original qualities, not for his resemblances to Montaigne.

Although our author's critics have always deplored the conditions of civil and religious strife in which Charron grew up and lived, they do not seem to have considered them when discussing

---

15 Supra, p. 17.

16 Supra, pp. 3, 42. Herbier, that is to say: botanist's collection of dried herbs.

17 Sabrié, *op. cit.,* p. 501.

18 *Ibid.,* pp. 529, 537.

19 Supra, p. 38.

20 Supra, p. 38.

21 Sabrié, *op. cit.,* p. 533.

22 *Ibid.,* pp. 531 f.

the development of his philosophy. I believe, however, that these conditions account for much that is similar in the *Sagesse* and the *Essays*; both authors reacted strongly to the disastrous picture offered them by the period.

We have seen how intimately Charron was associated with the counter-reformation in the Southwest, with such outstanding prelates as Arnaus de Pontac and Antoine Prevost de Sansac, two champions of the Council of Trent in France.

Excess was the general measure of the time, excess in politics, excess in religion, excess in the civil power's jurisdiction over the spiritual, and the cure of excess is moderation and self control. The *Trois Vérités,* although very successful, were the final experiment which showed our preacher that, even if he had been poised and calm in its writing, the answers would be violent and bitter and that before further attempts at discussion *un terrain d'entente* had to be found.[23] The *Sagesse* was to be this *terrain d'entente,* and we have shown how Charron proceeded to the formation of the *sage,* guiding him step by step to a *sagesse* which would then enable him to accept the *Trois Vérités.*

The *Sagesse* was directed to Protestants and Catholics alike. Charron was well aware that much of the Protestant criticism of the Catholics was deserved; he himself was an artisan of the counter-reformation. Many so-called Christians were Christians in name only and subsequently contributed to the deterioration of religion. We will show this later, when examining the unfinished proposed dedication of the *Discours Chrestien de la Divinité.*[24] The *Sagesse* was an invitation for all to strip themselves of false and superstitious belief and follow the path of prudence. Once moderation and self control have been attained, they would be capable of proceeding toward the true religion along the road offered by the *Trois Vérités.* The *Discours Chrestiens,* a treatment of the dogma, was intended to be the crowning achievement.

The true and important position of Montaigne in his period has always been recognised, and some of his critics, such as Villey and Strowsky, have pointed out the high esteem in which he was held by Huguenot and Catholic princes and the Kings.[25] Charron did

---

[23] Supra, pp. 92 ff.

[24] Infra, p. 122.

[25] Pierre Villey, *Les Sources et l'evolution des* Essais *de Montaigne,* 2 vols., Paris: Hachette, 1908.

not have the ear of Kings; he was, however, a man of great importance and renown in his own time.

We have shown how successful he quickly became as a preacher. His style was fresh, clear, and inspiring, and if he does not attain a classical style like that of Bossuet, he is, however, his only real precursor. A canon in many dioceses, an efficient administrator, a man entrusted with the post of *théologal* and *écolâtre,* he even beame the *Vicaire Général* of the bishop of Cahors, the highest position in the Church hierarchy up to that of bishop. Finally, he was truly esteemed and respected as is shown by the tone of Pierre de l'Estoile when he mentions his death:[26]

> Le dimanche 16e de ce mois, sur les onze heures du matin, tomba mort, en la rue S.-Jean-de-Beauvais, à Paris, M. Charron, homme d'Eglise et docte, comme ses escrits en font foi.

Even great personages unknown to him cared enough about him to invite him to join them for dinner when they heard of his presence in the same city. We find proof of this in two of his letters to La Rochemaillet dated the twenty-first of March, 1600 and the first of October, 1603 respectively, and written respectively from Bordeaux and Poitiers:

> En ceste ville sont Messieurs le Cardinal de Sourdys et d'Espernon qui me font très bonne chère; ... Monsieur le marquis de Villars estant icy arrivé hier soir, me vient d'envoyer convier pour souper par un gentilhomme, comme j'escrivais cecy. Je ne l'ay jamais veu ny luy moy, que je sache...[27]

A more intimate acquaintance of Pierre Charron was Montaigne. Even according to La Rochemaillet in his *Eloge,* they had become so close that the author of the *Essays,* willed our canon the right to wear his coat of arms. We have no proof of La Rochemaillet's statement, but it was made in writing in the *Eloge* and never disproved. Furthermore, the son-in-law of Montaigne, de Camain, was made by Charron administrator of his estate and residuary legatee

[26] Pierre de l'Estoile, *op. cit.,* vol. VIII, p. 107.
[27] Auvray, *op. cit.,* p. 321, 329.

and his wife, Mademoiselle de Montaigne, was to receive five hundred écus. This seems to show a certain intimacy between Charron and the Montaigne family.

We have never found, however, any mention of each other by either of our two authors in their works or in their letters; the *Catechisme* of Ochino is the only proof we have of a visit made by Charron to the Castle of Montàgne in 1586.[28]

All that we have said seems to point to a deep friendship on the intellectual plane between the two men, yet nothing shows any measurable influence of one on the other. To Montaigne, Charron was a great and remarkable preacher with whom he would enjoy timely discussions and conversations. To Charron the author of the *Essays* was the kind of man who shared his views on the troubled period in which they lived and was one of those rare noblemen who used his influence toward good ends, not simply to further his own interests.

We know from the essay *De l'Amitié* what Montaigne required of a friend and by the "De la Noblesse" of the *Sagesse* what was Charron's ideal of a nobleman. To the author of the essay *L'Art de Conférer,* nothing seems more agreeable than conversation[29] and his mind became fortified by practising it "avec des esprits vigoureux et réglez".[30] He feasts on and enjoys truth wherever he finds it. He has listened to the criticism made of his writings and has changed them accordingly, more "par raison de civilité que par raison d'amendement".[31]

Villey believes this essay was written around 1586 or 1587. This is the time of Charron's visit to Montaigne, which followed several years of acquaintance, and Charron seems to fit rather well the portrait of a conversationalist painted by the author of the *Essays.*

These years were also crucial years in the evolution of the "Moi" of the author of the *Essays.* Villey calls this period *la crise* and sees in it a change from stoïcism to a form of scepticism mildly mocking the weakness of humanity and the inadequacy of the stoïcism in which Montaigne once believed.

Villey had also noted that the 1588 and 1595 editions of the *Essays* show a mass introduction of quotations in Latin prose. Before then Montaigne always translated Latin prose and made it an

[28] Supra, p. 70.
[29] Montaigne, *op. cit.,* vol. III, p. 184.
[30] *Ibid.,* p. 185.
[31] *Ibid., p.* 187.

integral part of his text. The only quotations were verses used as added ornaments. Before 1588 Montaigne has about twenty quotations of Latin prose; after 1588 three hundred and forty new ones were added and in the 1595 edition[32] more than a thousand appeared.

We may wonder whether the "conferences" with Charron had anything to do with that change, since we know from his preface to the first edition of the *Sagesse* how Charron felt about quotations in Latin in his text:

> ... J'y ay parsemé de sentences latines, mais courtes et fortes... qui n'interrompent ny ne troublent le fil du texte Français. Car je n'ay peu encores estre induit à trouver meilleur de tourner telles allégations en Français (comme aucuns veulent) avec tel déchet et perte de la grace et énergie, qu'elles ont en leur naturel et original qui ne se peut jamais bien representer en autre langage.[33]

We have also noted the appearance of a certain scepticism or pyrrhonism in the work of Montaigne at that time. Already, then, Charron may have been interested in the advantages of scepticism applied to religion and in the safeguard of dogmas in religion, since a certain dose of pyrrhonism appears already in the first of the *Trois Vérités* and later in the *Sagesse*.

But the scepticism of Montaigne is an attitude, a post-dated warning he placed here and there in the *Essays* to make fun of the righteousness of the doctors, of human limitations, and of our inability to find absolute truth. Scepticism is very evident in the *Apologie de Raymond Sebond*; and it is there with a bitter laugh at this past disillusionment, quick as a whip, all through the *Essays*. It is an attitude of mind which does not try to draw conclusions.

For Charron, on the contrary, as we have shown, scepticism is a serious tool helping man "to know himself".[34] It is also the tool which helps the *sage* in securing a "universelle et plaine liberté de l'Esprit, tant en jugement qu'en volonté".[35] And this will lead to a conception which corresponds almost exactly to the scientific attitude accepted nowadays.

---

[32] Villey, *Sources*, vol. I, p. 510.
[33] Charron, *Sagesse*, 1607, p. 749.
[34] Supra, pp. 106 ff.
[35] Charron, *Sagesse*, 1607, p. 320.

The pyrrhonism of Charron is also limited. It does not touch dogma, but it is the foundation of the *Sagesse*. As soon as it has served the purpose, it is discarded and has no place in the strong construction of the moral of the *sage*. Descartes uses the same process in his *Discours de la Méthode*.[36]

The need for Charron's *Sagesse* and the intellectual and religious changes it implies is well shown in an unfinished epistle[37] which was to be the dedicatory introduction of the *Discours de la Divinité*. Published by La Rochemaillet in an unfinished and uncorrected form, this epistle clearly shows both what Charron wanted to fight and the aim of his new philosophy. The title speaks for itself. Our canon wants to discuss two sources of evils plaguing religious belief. One is minor and little felt, but hard to cure and to eradicate. It is superstition caused by exaggerated zeal or leftover paganism. People who where reared among these superstitions seem unable to keep their faith without them.

It would not be charitable for the *sage* to abandon these people to their foolish stubbornness. They should be shown the truth without being pushed or forced and some of them will follow the new path when they see it.

The second source of evil, and the worst of the two, is the lack of trust in God. The religious man knows and serves God, and serving depends upon knowing. "Si l'on mescognoit Dieu et que l'on le prenne pour autre qu'il n'est comme faict la plus part du monde, comment le pourra-t-on bien servir, adorer, prier."[38]

This, therefore, concerns most of the people, and Charron shows how each one has his own idea of God. The way they speak of Him, you would think it is of some "petit juge de village".

Some think of God as severe, quick to anger, hard to appease, exacting, watching them step by step, "les prenant au levé".[39] These know only fear. On the other hand, some believe Him to be easy, indulgent, too kind and only half aware of their doings. Therefore they behave nonchalantly in their religion and wonder if God will know about them or care. Some again (like the Tartuffe of Molière)

---

[36] Supra, p. 107.

[37] Bound with the 1645 edition of *De la Sagessė* by Feugé, we find the "Epistre, contenant, que les fautes qui se commettent au faict de la Religion, sont celles qui sont moins senties, et plus tard et plus malaisement corrigées et guaries, et que les plus grandes viennent de n'estimer et ne congnoistre pas Dieu comme il faut", p. 54.

[38] *Ibid.*, p. 56.

[39] *Ibid.*, p. 57.

have kind words and intentions but their souls are empty. They are only showing off to move others' opinions: "Car la religion est le vray champ de l'hypocrisie."[40]

Finally, some try to bargain with their Lord. They stipulate as conditions of their faith favors from Providence that they would be ashamed to ask in front of honorable men. Feeling that God should be satisfied with their service, they ask for the downfall of those who oppose them and pray only for their own material profit.

In a word, most of the believers do not go to God to learn to know Him and adore Him but to bring Him down to their pettiness by lending to the Divinity their own passions and limitations.

Charron concludes by deploring the fact that such a noble faith as the Christian faith had been disfigured by popular and shabby attitudes which destroy its early purity and simplicity. Too much emphasis has been placed on seeking to please the masses, when it was most important that the teaching from the pulpit show purity, simplicity and nobility as characterizing faith. But the worst evil of all is that most preachers have the same lowly conceptions and keep the fire of superstition and prejudice alive, or, even worse, help to light it themselves.

The numerous allusions by Pierre de l'Estoile, in his *Mémoires-Journaux,* to the violent kind of preaching heard in Paris during the League confirm Pierre Charron's statements on this subject.[41] Doubtless these criticisms of the sermons and preachers current in his time must have been expressed orally many times by Charron since he started his epistle with this assertion: "Monseigneur, ce sont deux mots entre autres que je dis volontiers en public et en privé..." This represents the way Charron felt about the religious belief of his contemporaries and shows clearly the purpose of the *Sagesse* as a foundation for a renewed and pure Catholic faith and as its best guarantee. We remember that the education of the *sage* is completed by the teaching of stoicism and this system of ethics will never permit the lowly attitudes toward the faith which were so strongly exposed and criticised by our preacher.

A last point should now be examined. Often the phrase "disciple de Montaigne" has been transformed to the "plagiaire et disciple de Montaigne",[42] and for some this plagiarism infers an intellectual dependence on the author of the *Essays.*

---

[40] *Ibid.,* p. 57.

[41] Pierre de l'Estoile, *op. cit.*

[42] Supra, pp. 38 ff.

Sabrié asserts in his studies of the sources of the *Sagesse* that Charron had borrowed from several authors more than he did from Montaigne. Huarte,[43] Justus-Lipsius, Bodin and Du Vair had furnished him with more material than Montaigne. Therefore Sabrié had accepted with a certain restriction the concept of Charron's dependency on Montaigne, although he had already stated that the thought of Montaigne lost only its literary appeal when studied in the *Sagesse*.[44] It therefore appears to us that Sabrié is contradicting himself, or perhaps we can assume that Sabrié was repeating in the latter statement what has always been said before without checking it with his own findings.

Sabrié was using the edition[45] of the *Sagesse* published by Amaury Duval[46] in the *Collection des Moralistes Français*. This edition was published *avec des commentaires et de nouvelles notices biographiques*; the footnotes are mainly there to point out the Latin sources of the *Sagesse*. From time to time Duval's footnotes refer to the *Essays* as the source of a particular passage. He is altogether too hasty and too unprecise in these references, and this is too bad; they certainly contributed much to affect the subsequent criticism of the *Sagesse*, although Sabrié is the only one to mention he had used this particular and late edition of the *Sagesse*.

Delboulle in his article "Charron Plagiaire de Montaigne"[47] studied again most of the passages of the *Sagesse* that Duval had pointed out as passages taken from the *Essays*; however Delboulle refers only to a 1782 edition of the *Sagesse* "suivant la vraie copie de Bourdeaux". In his article Delboulle compares the text of the *Sagesse* to the so-called text source of the *Essays*.

We can classify Duval's and Delboulle's references to the *Essays* as sources of the *Sagesse* into three categories:

1. The first is made of typical sentences or quotations, almost proverbs, or the type of maxim used in sermons as introduction or conclusion to a point well made; as for instance: "Chascun appelle barbarie ce qui n'est de son goust et usage."[48] For this passage both Duval and Delboulle refer their reader to the *Essays*, Vol. I, Ch.

---

[43] Supra, p. 43.

[44] Sabrié, *op. cit.*, p. 4.

[45] *Ibid.*, p. 26.

[46] Pierre Charron, *De la Sagesse*, 3 vols., Amaury Duval edition, *Collection des moralistes Français*, vol. VII, VIII, IX, Paris: Chassériau, 1821.

[47] *RHL*, vol. VII, 1900, p. 284.

[48] *Sagesse* by Duval, vol. II, p. 57, Delboulle, *op. cit.*, p. 290.

XXX, which is the essay "Des Cannibales", Vol. I, Ch. XXXI, in Villey's edition. It appears there in the following form: "... sinon que chacun appelle barbarie ce qui n'est pas de son usage."[49] Here are some others of these passages:

> La cérémonie nous deffend d'exprimer les choses naturelles et licites et nous l'en croyons: la nature et la raison nous defend les illicites et personne ne l'en croit.[50]

> Repentance est un désaveu et un desdit de la volonté.[51]

It should be noticed that this maxim type of sentence is usually followed by many others not found in the *Essays* and sometimes traced back by Duval to their Latin sources. This should remind us of the scores of compilations of sayings, maxims and odd customs available in a strangely mingled confusion to the sixteenth-century reader hungry for general information and fact which would enable him to attempt to form for himself a sensible opinion of humanity.

We find this notion expressed often in the small summaries preceding each essay in Villey's edition of the *Essays*. In his *Sources et Evolution des Essais de Montaigne*,[52] Villey had already insisted on this idea and gave a list of the compilers, mainly interested in the customs of marriage, he had come across just by chance during his readings.

2. The second category embodied imprecise references to the *Essays* by Duval. He says for instance: "Charron a emprunté ce trait comme beaucoup d'autres qu'il cite dans ce chapitre, de Montaigne, L I, Ch XXII"[53] or elsewhere: "Charron mutile ici de très belles Pensées de Montaigne"[54] or again:

> ... Il fallait dire, femme de Xercès. Mais Charron qui copie ici Montaigne a fait la même faute que lui. Amyot a le premier trompé Montaigne, en mettant par inadvertance le mot de mère dans le *Traité de la Superstition*, traduit de Plutarque.

---

[49] Montaigne, *op. cit.*, p. 265.

[50] Delboulle, *op. cit.*, p. 291, Duval refers us to Cicero for this passage. *Sagesse* by Duval, vol. II, p. 91.

[51] Delboulle, *op. cit.*, p. 291.

[52] Villey, *Sources*, vol. II, p. 189.

[53] *Sagesse* by Duval, vol. II, p. 204.

[54] *Ibid.*, p. 141.

I fail to see why Charron would have made from the *Essays* the two borrowings just mentioned when they are mainly citations from Cicero and Plutarch, both of whom have been mentioned many times by Duval as sources for Charron. Here identical sources for Montaigne and Charron would seem to be a fairer critical conclusion.

3. In the third category belong principally several passages of greater length cited by both Duval and Delboulle, or by Delboulle alone, as having been inspired by the *Essays.* They resemble the so-called models only in part and usually when examples or particularities are cited to illustrate a point or a theory. A number of these passages (ten to be exact, plus six which should be entered in the first category described above) belong to the *Apologie de Raimond Sebond,* where Montaigne defends natural theology and shows the weakness of human reason and the vanity of science.

I have checked some of the sources of Montaigne's *Essays* in the Villey edition and I have found that most of them are Lucretius, Pliny, Amyot's Plutarch, Seneca and some of the popular compilations of the time.[55] Many of these are "star entries" which means that Villey has judged them to be so close to the attributable text of their sources that they were more than simple reminiscences of the well furnished memory of the widely read author of the *Essays.* It goes without saying that all this material was also available to Charron.

From the three volumes of the *Sagesse* Delboulle has cited seventy passages he believed could be traced to the *Essays.* We should point out here that these passages, taken in the order they are found in the *Sagesse,* come from many places throughout the *Essays* and do not follow each other in any chronological order except for eight passages from the *Apologie de Raimond Sebond.* These eight passages constitute a different case we will study later by itself.[56]

We have therefore sixty-two passages of an average length of twenty-five words, similar as to their text but dissimilar in regard to their use in the general plan of the respective works where they appeared in the form of quotations and illustrations.

Considering the preceding and the fact we have shown that both Charron and Montaigne were well acquainted with the same sources of material (Latin authors, translations from Greek, compilations),

---

[55] Montaigne, *op. cit.,* vol. III, pp. 485 ff.

[56] Infra, pp. 128 ff.

we feel that the long-harboured belief that Charron plagiarized Montaigne should be abandoned. Charron read the *Essays*, and as a humanist always anxious "de se meubler l'esprit" might have jotted down some of the stimulating thoughts he found there and added them to his gleanings from other authors. There is no reason to believe he did more than this, for when he did any borrowing of consequence he tells us so, as we will see.

Among the humanists borrowing was a current practice, and the author of the *Sagesse*, like his friend Montaigne, thought it useless to repeat under another form what had already been well said. However, the use of this material in the construction of one's work does not mean that this work is a reproduction or a re-edition of the sources, although it may be an effort to prop one's own philosophical edifice with known and accepted works. This is what our author means when he declares in his preface:

> J'adjouste icy deux ou trois mots de bonne foy: l'un que j'ai questé par-cy par-là la plus part des matériaux de cet ouvrage des meilleurs autheurs qui ont traicté cette matière politique et morale, vraye science de l'homme, tant anciens... que modernes. C'est le recueil d'une partie de mes estudes; la forme et l'ordre sont à moy.[57]

Later in a small preface preceding his chapter discussing "De la Prudence politique du Souverain pour gouverner estats" Charron praises Lipsius' treatment of this subject and adds "La moëlle de son livre est icy".[58]

The same acknowledgment goes to Du Vair in an *Advertissement* preceding the treatment of the "Passions en general". He has used the short moral treatise of Du Vair because he said: "...et n'ay point veu qui les dépeigne plus naïvement et richement."[59]

Montaigne himself did some borrowing from contemporary authors. For instance, Villey showed the resemblance of the *Apologie de Sebond* to the Quod nihil scitur of Sánchez from the University of Toulouse.[60] He also pointed out that Montaigne borrowed for the same essay some passages from the *Trois Dialogues contre*

[57] Charron, *Sagesse*, 1607, p. 748.
[58] *Ibid.*, pp. 485 f.
[59] *Ibid.*, p. 111.
[60] Villey, *Sources*, vol. II, p. 167.

les nouveaux Academiciens of Guy de Bruès.[61] It would be ridiculous and absurd, however, to conclude from this that Montaigne was a plagiarist or a disciple of Bruès or of Sánchez, yet this conclusion has been drawn again and again in the case of Charron and Montaigne.

Now it would be interesting to note here that Villey formulated a conjecture to explain in this year 1576 similarities in the simultaneous sceptical writings of Sánchez' *Quod nihil scitur* and Montaigne's *Apologie de Raimond Sebond*: "Peut-être à Bordeaux, ou à Toulouse, y avait-il un petit foyer de scepticisme, peut-être tous deux ont-ils reçu une même excitation au scepticisme...?"[62] This is the year 1576, and Charron had been near Bordeaux since 1572.[63] He had just received his doctorat in Montpellier in 1571,[64] and Sánchez was in Montpellier as a student and later as a teacher between his departure from Bordeaux in 1569 and his establishment in Toulouse in 1575.[65] Could Charron be that "même excitation au scepticisme" about which Villey is inquiring?

All we know is that there are coincidences and that these coincidences are inescapable. Villey tells us that Montaigne and Sánchez belong to the same age, that the evolution of their thoughts have the same beginning and that they are manifestations of their environment. This is also true in the case of Charron and should explain even better why Delboulle has found these eight similar passages we have mentioned[66] between the chapter of the *Sagesse* "Seconde considération de l'homme, qui est par comparaison de luy avec tous les autres animaux"[67] and the *Apologie de Raimond Sebond* in the *Essays*.

We can conclude, as did Villey in the case of Montaigne,[68] that in this part of the *Sagesse*, as in the *Apologie de Raimond Sebond*, and as in many contemporary works, we find compilations of opinions on the nature of the soul and on prime principles. They are almost identical from one work to another, always tending to

---

[61] *Ibid.*, p. 172.

[62] *Ibid.*, p. 169.

[63] Supra, p. 64.

[64] Supra, p. 62.

[65] Villey, *Sources*, vol. II, p. 168.

[66] Supra, p. 124.

[67] Ch. VIII, vol. I in 1601 edition, or Ch. XXIV, p. 151 in the 1607 edition of the *Sagesse*.

[68] Villey, *Sources*, vol. II, p. 171.

establish the inability of human reason to know itself and to isolate the prime elements of things.

From all of these various considerations it follows that the assertion that Charron was walking in the steps of Montaigne by re-editing the *Essays* in his *Sagesse* is without foundation. It has been all along essentially an inherited opinion which was allowed to go unchallenged. Furthermore, this effort to fit the criticism of Charron to the already existing pattern sometimes yields strange results and distorts some of the facts.

As we have seen, Charron had once put "a foot into the League",[69] but having quickly understood his mistake, he had courageously attacked the League and the Sorbonne for inciting the subjects of the Kingdom to revolt. But Strowski, who sees in Charron a disciple of Montaigne, goes into an elaborate explanation to show that this is a turning point in Charron's life and a reason for Charron to call Montaigne's stoicism to the aid of his failing judgment.[70] And Strowski concludes erroneously that when Montaigne was not satisfied with stoicism alone and called to his help the scepticism of Pyrrho, Charron did the same.

We know, however, that Charron first uses scepticism[71] as a tool for the foundation of his *Sagesse* and then stoicism as a training school for his *sage*. Consequently, there is a difference between Charron's moral system and that of Montaigne. Strowski is forced to admit this difference, but explains it by stating that "le doute de Montaigne était inspiré par l'humanité et la bonté; ... celui de Charron est inspiré par l'orgueil."[72] Strowski does not see that Charron's scepticism is for him the first step towards the acquisition of a prudent wisdom. Falsely he accuses him of being "le moins démocrate des hommes", quoting excerpts from the *Sagesse* to this effect, when Charron was in fact trying to show that a sceptical attitude would help his *sage* to rid himself of popular superstitions and to avoid some of the regrettable and tragic popular excesses so often witnessed during the war of religions.

As we have shown before, so sudden and unexplained a turning point as seen by Strowski could not exist in the life of our preacher

[69] Supra, p. 88.
[70] Strowsky, *op. cit.*, p. 179.
[71] Supra, p. 121.
[72] Strowsky, *op. cit.*, p. 161.

and distinguished humanist.[73] If we have called attention again to this particular fact it is to show once more how the criticism of Charron has been hampered by the concept of his intellectual affiliation with the author of the *Essays.*

---

[73] *Ibid.*, p. 58.

Chapter VII

CONCLUSION

For almost three and one half centuries Pierre Charron has been referred to as the "disciple de Montaigne" or as his "secrétaire", and the general impression which his critics have left is that his moral treatise, the *Sagesse*, was largely inspired by the *Essays*.

We have surveyed the criticism on Charron and have found three distinct trends in that criticism.

The first trend was represented by the French Protestants' criticism of the *Trois Vérités*. It consisted essentially of small pamphlets concerned primarily with vindicating the Protestant movement and attacking its new opponent, Pierre Charron and his *troisième vérité*, which showed that the Catholic Church was the only true Church. As the fever of religious polemic which had accompanied the religious wars died out, this type of criticism came to an end and had no continuator. Our author had quickly seen the futility of his efforts to defend his third *vérité* against the violent partisan and polemic writings of the Protestants. He had understood the need for a basic understanding of a philosophy of life before proceeding any further with his plan for a third edition of the *Trois Vérités*, and his *De la Sagesse* was his offering towards that goal.

In the next generation there were two opposed factions in the criticism of the *Sagesse*, and these are responsible for the second and third trends in the criticism of Charron. These two sets of people, whose ideas are opposed to one another, had one thing in common: they both distorted Charron's thought to fit their own purposes.

The *libertins* lifted out of the *Sagesse* passages, which, when removed from their contexts, would seem to support their rationalistic pursuits; since then these ideas have been dubbed intellectual *libertinage*. They chose to disregard Charron's ultimate spiritual purpose which was so often expressed in the *Sagesse* and which could never be doubted because of his *Trois Vérités* and his *Discours Chrétiens*.

Father Mersenne and Father Garasse, in opposition to the *libertins*, fought Charron on account of the use the *libertins* made of his *Sagesse*. In their effort to score over their adversaries, the two priests felt it was necessary to discredit the authority the *libertins* quoted and praised so often. They attacked Charron, quoting him out of context as the *libertins* had done, and chose to disregard his intentions and the part the *Sagesse* was to have in his program. Concurring in the same ideas, we find Fathers Garasse and Mersenne coining the expression *sécrétaire* or *petit disciple* of Montaigne and applying it to Charron to further their attempt to knock the idol of the *libertins* from his pedestal. This was done in an effort to divorce Charron from the environment which had created him as a thinker and which had subsequently been influenced by him.

Along with the end of the religious wars, the early years of the seventeenth century witnessed the birth of our modern age. A few men molded the modern mind through their works, their actions, and their influence—Montaigne and Charron were two of them.

Their moral systems were different, even though their goals were similar, and they drew from the same material in their humanistic culture. If the rationalistic *libertins* preferred the *Sagesse* with its clear-cut symmetry to the more artistic *Essays*, it was because Charron offered to the searching generation which followed him a rationalistic system of morals, whereas Montaigne limited his readers to an excursion into their "self" with a true appraisal of their judgment and experience.

Therefore, when Mersenne and Garasse made of Charron a *disciple of Montaigne* they attempted to suppress a new school of thought which had found its source in Charron. They were quite successful in deliberately misinterpreting Charron's real meaning and purpose, and in discrediting him as an independent thinker since their interpretation has been the only one to survive in the history of criticism on Charron.

While it is true that in recent times Charron has always been mentioned, and sometimes prominently, in studies on rationalism and religious thought in France, this recognition has been subjected to the always accepted but never demonstrated premise that Charron was the *disciple of Montaigne* and that he had, in an orderly fashion, faithfully rearranged the ideas of the *Essays* in his *Sagesse*.

Consequently, according to this erroneous interpretation, any of Charron's influence on the following generation was attributed to Montaigne.

Sabrié and Busson felt, as Bonnefon had, that they needed to offer some apology for bothering their readers with their discussions of Charron and invariably stated that their work was useful since Charron had been the friend and the disciple of Montaigne, and that to study the *Sagesse* was to study an herbarium where you could find duly catalogued and classified the thoughts of Montaigne.

We have seen how the partisan criticism of Charron by Mersenne and Garasse has still survived in our modern literary criticism, but Garasse and Mersenne would hardly be considered impartial sources with which to begin a study of Charron. In the middle of the seventeenth century, however, we have found that Charles Sorel, in an attempt to give the first objective and unbiased criticism of our canon, presented in his *Bibliothèque Françoise* the two diametrically opposed opinions which were then current about the *Sagesse,* but unfortunately, because of certain tactics, one opinion became preponderant and this is how Mersenne's and Garasse's criticism on Charron became so influential in later periods.

When French literary criticism found a renewed interest in the influential thinkers of the late French Renaissance, Saint-Beuve began at the place at which Charles Sorel had left off. Sainte-Beuve was shocked by the fact that some *beaux esprits* had found Charron equal or superior to Montaigne and subsequently devoted himself to proving that the *Sagesse* is nothing but "une édition didactique des Essais, une table bien raisonnée des matières" and that literary criticism should place its author in the shadow of Montaigne.[1]

Sainte-Beuve, who is now considered more of a moralist than a critic, drew this opinion directly or indirectly from the moralist Garasse, who had called the *Sagesse* a poorly thought-out translation of the *Essays* by Montaigne's little secretary, Charron. Present-day critics and authors of literary histories have left Charron where Garasse and Sainte-Beuve placed him: behind Montaigne, "Charron son disciple le suit pas à pas".

Sabrié did a very remarkable work in gathering and analysing all that had been said about Charron and the *Sagesse* up to 1913. His evaluation of Garasse's criticism on Charron is exhaustive, and

[1] Sainte-Beuve, *op. cit.,* p. 269.

the conclusions he draws are persuasive. There is no doubt, and these are Sabrié's own words, that "Garasse's accusations are only calumny".[2] Yet Sabrié has still accepted Garasse's firm and enduring theory, handed down to him by Sainte-Beuve and Faguet, that in the *Sagesse* we find the thought of Montaigne in a dried-up form. Sabrié accepted this theory without any doubt; in one of the several places where he quoted Faguet about it he tells us, "On peut dire que 'Charron c'est l'herbier de Montaigne', ou, si l'on veut, que la *Sagesse*, ce sont les *Essais* mis en ordre";[3] and we have shown how Sabrié seems to be in contradiction with himself on this point when he discusses the sources of the *Sagesse*.

This concept of literary affiliation between Montaigne and Charron is deceptive and has had a completely misleading effect on criticism of Charron. Always accepted by the best of our critics, this concept caused unnecessary puzzlement about evident contradictions between the "master" and his "disciple". Nevertheless, they endeavored to make Charron fit into this concept.

We have already pointed out some of the contradictions or explanations that Sabrié uses in order to remain within the limits of this concept. Here is another: "Montaigne a l'air plu vieilli que Charron, et c'est pour cela qu'il est moins goûté que son disciple."[4]

Busson, following the same path, said: "Charron c'est un Montaigne, mais un Montaigne qui aurait de l'ordre, ... qui aurait même un système cohérent, un Montaigne qui serait devenu dogmatique."[5]

Many critics have been led to the unwarranted conclusion, by following this same concept, that the *Sagesse* is a re-edition of the *Essays*. Strowski, for instance, stated that Charron obtained his ideas on the education of children from Montaigne's *Essays*, and Sabrié later found that Charron drew them from Huarte's *Examen de Ingenios para las Ciencias*.[6] Furthermore, we should note here that in his extensive and exhaustive study of the sources of the *Essays* Villey tells us on two different occasions that he has never found any proof which could lead him to believe that Montaigne had read Huarte's work.[7]

---

[2] Sabrié, *op. cit.*, pp. 478-485.
[3] *Ibid.*, p. 271.
[4] *Ibid.*, p. 491.
[5] Busson, *op. cit.*, p. 181.
[6] Supra, p. 43.
[7] Villey, *Sources*, vol. II, pp. 314.

Moreover, it seems that this generally accepted concept of Charron's literary affiliation with Montaigne prompted Villey to state that Montaigne's ideas on conversation were spread during the seventeenth century as much by the *Sagesse* as by the *Essays*, since in the *Sagesse* " 'cet herbier de Montaigne'... on voit Charron ratisser en un ou deux chapitres toutes les sentences que Montaigne avait semées çà et là dans son livre sur le sujet de la conversation".[8]

Certainly Villey made this statement in good faith, since, like all the other critics, he accepted as a prerequisite that the *Sagesse* was the herbarium of Montaigne. However, it seems quite unbelievable that the four pages of the chapter, "Se bien comporter avec autruy", where Charron teaches his *sage* the art of "commune conversation" and of "conversation plus spéciale",[9] could be found here and there in the *Essays* in isolated phrases. First, this would have been a long and a tedious process for Charron to use in composing his *Sagesse*, and we should keep in mind that he expected to have it finished in three months. That it actually took him a little less than three years[10] can be explained by the fact that the work proved to be much more extensive than he had originally planned. Also, during this time he was kept very busy by his bishop, who entrusted to him, his *vicaire général*, "tout le soin de son clergé".[11] Furthermore, Montaigne had written a celebrated essay "De l'art de conférer" from which, if this were the case, we would expect Charron to have derived some ideas. However, I could not find any similarity between Charron's text and Montaigne's. Furthermore we find that Delboulle in the article we have cited previously makes no mention of any similarity on this point between the two writers. We remember that Duval in his edition of the *Sagesse* always mentions the slightest resemblance to the *Essays*, and in this chapter, "Se bien comporter avec autruy", he points out that one sentence ("C'est un plaisir face [sic.] affaire à gens qui cèdent, flattent et applaudissent") is "Paroles de Montaigne, L. III, Ch. VIII".[12] The only sentence similar to Charron's which can be found in the essay, "L'Art de conférer", is "C'est un plaisir fade et nuisible d'avoir affaire à

---

[8] Villey,*Sources*, vol. II, pp. 366-367.

[9] Charron, *Sagesse*, 1607, p. 488.

[10] Auvray, *op.cit.*, pp. 307 ff.

[11] *Ibid.*, p. 308.

[12] Charron, *Sagesse*, by Duval, p. 218.

gens qui nous admirent et facent place".[13] Duval's comment is therefore deceptive and Villey's statement seems groundless.

If we add to these considerations the conclusions we drew after we had discussed the full significance of the charge brought against Charron —that he had plagiarized the *Essays*—, we are forced to recognize that the claim that Charron was the disciple of Montaigne was never substantiated. Despite the fact that it has never been proved, it has been unhappily the premise on which new theories of criticism on Charron have been built.

We have pointed out that all evidence seems to show that Garasse was the originator of this concept which became his best psychological weapon in his polemics against Charron. With all the absurd calumnies formulated against Charron by the Jesuit, his main target was the *Sagesse,* and his main objective was not Charron's reputation, but the esteem in which his fellow Frenchmen of the seventeenth century held the *Sagesse,* because that esteem had made it one of the best sellers of the moment. In this effort Garasse scored a victory, because, when the belief that Charron was the disciple of Montaigne and the *Sagesse* a flavorless re-edition of the *Essays* became generally accepted, the reading public then concentrated its interest on the *Essays.* After this the *Sagesse* became only a curiosity, because, to use again Sainte-Beuve's own words: some "Beaux esprits, médiocres juges en cela"[14] had found its author equal or superior to Montaigne.

In this Garasse had shown himself to be the champion of the old "esprit de Sorbonne" which had been Charron's life-long enemy. Charron was of the new school and was in complete agreement with the new bishops (who where among the most brilliant humanists of the century) chosen by Francis I and the Popes. We recall how the Sorbonne, faithful to the centuries-old tradition, systematically opposed all the movements of the new order. As the new canon and *théologal* of the young bishop Arnaus de Pontac, a humanist of distinction, Charron assumed the job of supervising the teaching of theology in the Southwest, and Charron had never studied theology at the Sorbonne or at any other university. From the beginning therefore, Charron personified to the doctors of the Sorbonne the new system of theology.

---

[13] Montaigne, *op. cit.,* vol. III, p. 188.

[14] Supra, p. 38.

Pierre Charron could also defeat the doctors of the Sorbonne on their own grounds. He showed us in his *Lettre à un Docteur de Sorbonne* that a subject cannot ever make legitimate a rebellion against his King, and he publicly castigated the Sorbonne for taking part in the revolt against Henry III at the time of the League.

Although the doctors of the Sorbonne never dared to answer Charron on the touchy question of the subject's allegiance to the King, they did their utmost to raise all possible obstacles in the path of our canon and to ruin his reputation. For lack of a better term Charron called these archenemies of his "Les pédants",[15] and with Garasse these *pédants,* doctors of the Sorbonne, were responsible for the deliberate misinterpretations of the *Sagesse* after its 1601 edition. In 1602 Charron had tried in vain through the good offices of his friend La Rochemaillet and of Monsieur de Boulogne to obtain from two doctors of the Sorbonne an official approbation for the second edition of the *Sagesse.*[16]

When Charron found that the doctors could not be coaxed into accepting the *Sagesse* for what it was, a treatise on human moderation and prudence, and not a treatise on religious morals, he decided to answer them in both the new preface to his next edition of the *Sagesse*[17] and the small *Traicté de Sagesse* which we have specially studied.

Charron's death did not disarm the Sorbonne, and we have seen that his friend La Rochemaillet had to overcome many difficulties before the publication of the second edition of the *Sagesse* was finally authorised. In his *Eloge* La Rochemaillet gave a few details describing all the machinery which was set in motion to stop the publication of Charron's work, and, later, to have the printed *Sagesse* impounded or banned. The matter was settled only when the Attorney-General ordered two doctors of the Sorbonne to put in writing their complaints about the *Sagesse* and then turned the

---

[15] Charron, *Sagesse,* 1607, preface, p. 15.

[16] Auvray, *op. cit.,* p. 323, 326, and 327.

[17] In the conclusion of this preface Charron says of the detractors at whom he is aiming (the doctors of the Sorbonne):

> Que si encores apres tout, il ne se contente et ne l'approuve, qu'il l'attaque hardiment et vivement (car de mes-dire seulement, de mordre, et charpenter le nom d'autruy, il est assés aysé, mais trop indigne et trop pédant) il aura tost ou une franche confession et acquiescement, car ce livre fait gloire et feste de bonne foy, et de l'ingenuité: ou un examen de son impertinence et folie.

Sagesse, 1607, p. 22.

whole thing over to President Jeannin, Conseiller d'Estat. The latter, once he realized how much of an asset the *Sagesse* was for cultivated people, recommended to the King's private Council that they lift the ban which had been imposed upon it.[18]

Therefore La Rochemaillet, with the intervention of enlightened people, was able to score a last victory for Charron against the old *esprit de Sorbonne.* A few decades later Mersenne and Garasse were very successful in renewing the old fight over the *Sagesse,* as I have shown. Successful, but in an indirect way, and Charron and his *Sagesse* sank into relative oblivion, not because of the frontal attacks and slanderous accusations of the opposition, but because they had reduced our canon to the rank of a "secretary to Montaigne".

This need not have happened, as Pierre Charron had foreseen that his *Sagesse* would be misinterpreted by the hypocrites and by the ignorant and coarse *pédant,* or, one might say, the *libertins* and the censors of the Sorbonne. This is why a few months before his death he had written the *Petit Triacté de Sagesse* in which he gave, in addition to an abstract of his *Sagesse,* a defense answering complaints and objections and a declaration of intention. Garasse and all those who followed his path probably knew of this *Traicté,* but it didn't suit their purpose to take it into consideration. Truly, if they had, their attacks against the *Sagesse* would not have seemed motivated any longer and Pierre Charron might now occupy the place he deserves in the history of French literary criticism. In the later periods, as I said when I discussed the *Traicté* at length, Charron's critics have always neglected this little piece; when they do mention it, they dismiss it as a little digest of the *Sagesse* followed by a short polemic.

To win over the Sorbonne required a man of importance, and Charron was every inch that kind of a man. I have pointed out that before assuming a place in the history of rationalism Pierre Charron occupied in his own lifetime a prominent position in the Church of France, and his achievements in the performance of his many duties and the fashion in which he shouldered great and delicate responsibilities were well known. Thus it is easy to understand why Claude Dormy, Bishop of Boulogne and Prior of Saint-Martin-des-Champs in Paris, tried so persistently to persuade Charron to accept the position of *théologal* under him.[19] The bishop

---

[18] Charron, *Sagesse,* 1607, *Eloge,* p. X.

[19] Charron, *Sagesse,* 1607, *Eloge,* p. VII.

wanted, La Rochemaillet tells us, to keep Charron close to the court, where, already in the early 1600's, the best talents and the best minds mingled.

From all that has been said of the great success and popularity of Charron's sermons, there seems to be no doubt that he was one of the greatest preachers of his time. To this achievement we should add the great merit due Charron for having been the artisan of the Catholic counter-reform in the Southwest. Here he worked with the young prelates of humanistic training who had set themselves the task of carrying through in their dioceses the program of reforms of the Council of Trent and who helped persuade the rest of the French bishops to follow their example. The General Assembly of the Clergy of France in 1595 had as a main objective the application of the decrees of the Council of Trent. These decrees, as will be recalled, never acquired the power of law in France, and consequently any compliance was a matter of professional and moral integrity, as such compliance was never publicized for fear of the Gallican opposition of the Parlements and of the Sorbonne. This explains why Charron's critics have never mentioned or noticed Charron's achievements in this particularly sensitive field of the Catholic counter-reform. However, these achievements were remarkable enough for our canon to deserve the honor, not only of becoming the Southwest's representative at the Assembly, but also of being elected its first secretary.

Pierre Charron unquestionably had achieved recognized leadership. The great and immediate success of his works, sold out as soon as they were published, furnishes us with an additional proof of this, and it becomes untenable that such a man would have to look up to a contemporary to find a philosophy in which he could find inspiration. If Charron was good enough to inspire his contemporaries by his sermons or by his pen, the source of the inspiration prompting him had to be in his inner self, and not in some other person.

In the same fashion, the *Essays* and the *Sagesse* offer two entirely different philosophies to any reader, and a man of the 1600's found different lessons in the two works. Montaigne had chosen the essay in preference to any other form, because it gave him complete freedom of action and he could, as he said, "suivre son humeur".[20] The *Essays* went through three stages. They follow

[20] Villey, *Sources*, vol. I, p. 36.

first the form of lessons intended for the popularisation of science and knowledge. Then, after the *crise stoicienne* and the *crise sceptique,* they become successively an investigation of his personal judgment and experience and a means of studying his "self". In all, the system of morals offered by the *Essays* is an indirect consequence of the fact that Montaigne was able to derive from his humanistic readings a normal and sane *modus vivendi* in face of the daily occurrence of the unpleasant excesses caused by the religious wars and the political situation.

On the contrary, Charron's philosophy offers a system of morals, but his system is not a by-product of his *De la Sagesse* but is self-contained in the *De la Sagesse* itself. It is intended not merely as a sane *modus vivendi* to teach Charron's readers how to live with the difficulties of the time, but to insufflate in them the *sagesse humaine* as the necessary base for making the reception of the *Trois Vérités* possible and fruitful. We find scepticism and stoicism in the *Sagesse,* not under the form of "crisis", but as tools masterfully manipulated by Charron to create the foundation of *sagesse* in the souls of his disciples and to give them proper philosophical training.

Reading Charron's *Sagesse* can often be quite inspiring if you can only allow yourself to follow the reasoning of the author on the ground he is clearing for you. A good example of this is found in the fifth chapter of the second book of the *Sagesse.* The area is clear, the foundations are laid, the time has come to build and "de dresser les règles de *sagesse,* dont la première et plus noble regarde la religion, et service de Dieu. La Piétié tient le premier lieu au rang de nos devoirs..."[21] The title of the chapter is therefore: "Estudier à la vraye piété, premier office de *sagesse*". Charron deplores the fact that there are so many religions, all pretending to be the true one, and often trying to assert their truth by cruel and inhuman practices and sacrifices, all reproaching the others for their shortcomings, all deploring, condemning and rejecting the others' erroneousness. Reminding his readers that, as he shows it in his *Trois Vérités,* the Christian religion is the only true and authentic religion, he states: "C'est le sujet de ma seconde vérité, où est monstré combien toutes les autres demeurent au dessous d'elle".[22]

[21] Charron, *Sagesse,* 1607, p. 380.
[22] *Ibid.,* p. 384.

We should note here that Charron uses the present tense, and not the past. Therefore he writes this keeping very much present, and as an attainment the truth of the Christian Religion. He is certainly not, as it is so often repeated, undermining the foundations of the Christian faith, thinking that he can do so safely, because he had already been its apologist in the *Trois Vérités*.

To present a very definite proof, it was necessary to gather all the evidence generally available to his contemporaries, and to knit it into his demonstration of true piety, and this without leaving any holes or weakness in the proof. Every argument that the adversaries could use had to be included in the disputation. The lawyer as well as the preacher reappear here. Again, this is not *libertinage* for Charron to state that "Toutes les religions ont cela, qu'elles sont estranges et horribles au sens commun"[23] because their foundations are usually too "basses, indignes et messéantes" or too "hautes, esclatantes, miraculeuses et mystérieuses. *Praedicamus Jesum Crucifixum, Judaeis scandalum, gentibus stultitiam.*" The human mind is such that in its appraisal of its own capability of judging in matters of religion it would lean either way but certainly not recognize its limitation and accept it purely and simply. Recognition of the need for God's grace in this matter does not make of Charron a *libertin.* Here he is following to the letter the teaching of his Church.

Charron continues his demonstration. The fact is that if true religion finds its source in divine revelation, in each individual case one's religion is determined by one's place of birth and environment. "...L'on est circonsis, baptisé, Juif et Chrestien, avant que l'on scache que l'on est homme"; however the "vrays et bons professeurs[24] d'icelles, outre la profession externe qui est commune à tous, voire et aux mescroyants, ont le don de Dieu, le témoignage du S. Esprit au dedans".[25] The tribulations of Christendom are good proof of that.

Then Charron rises vehemently against those for whom faith was no more than an external attitude. Let us be reminded that the multiple abjurations of Henry IV were far from being an exception. For many in the preceding decades religion had been only an instrument to achieve a political aim. We have shown this when we discussed Charron and his age.

---

[23] *Ibid.*, p. 384.

[24] Professor of a faith.

[25] Charron, *Sagesse*, 1607, p. 387.

The superstitious do not fare any better under our canon's pen. Their so-called piety is but false religion. "Il n'y a rien qui fasse plus belle mine et prenne plus de peine à ressembler la vraye piété et religion; mais qui lui soit plus contraire et ennemie que la superstition: comme le loup qui ne ressemble pas trop mal le chien..."

Charron's style reaches great eloquence as he becomes more indignant with the evil perpetrated by the superstitious. Their attitude comes from the fact they do not think God worthy enough, they bring Him down to their level, they judge Him using themselves as models, they lend Him their humors and blasphemies. Still worse, however, are those who use superstition to achieve their ambition. Among the great and powerful some permit and cultivate superstition, although they know very well they should not, because they can use it as a tool to achieve their own aim. They will go even further and "...en forgent et inventent de nouvelles".[26]

Charron teaches us that religion is to know God and ourselves, to raise God to the highest while humbling ourselves and thus finding in God refuge and shelter for our nothingness. The result of religion should be honor and glory for God and profit for us. God is the last effort of our imagination's reaching toward perfection, or more exactly, God is infinitely above all the ultimate and highest efforts of our imagination's reaching toward perfection.[27]

In the conclusion of this inspiring exhortation Charron shows again that his *Sagesse* is the tool which prepares the ground of the *sage's* soul for the reception of the *Trois Vérités,* the proof of the true religion.

> Voila sommairement pour la piété, laquelle doit estre en premiére recommandation, contemplant toujours Dieu d'une ame franche, allègre et filiale, non effarouchée ny troublée, comme les supersticieux. Pour les particularitez, tant de la créance qu'observance il se faut tenir à la Chrestienne, comme la vraye, plus riche, plus relevée, plus honorable à Dieu, profitable et consolative à l'homme, ainsi qu'avons monstré en nostre seconde vérité, et en icelle demeurant, il faut d'une douce submission et obéïssance s'en remettre et arrester à ce que l'Eglise Catholique a de tout

---

[26] Charron, *Sagesse,* 1607, p. 387.
[27] Charron, *Sagesse,* 1607, p. 394.

> temps universellement tenu et tient, sans disputer et s'embrouiller en nouveauté ou opinion triée et particulière pour les raisons déduites en nostre troisième vérité spécialement ès premier et dernier chapitres, qui suffiront à celuy qui ne pourra ou ne voudra lire tout le livre.[28]

There can not be any doubt, religion is the last complement to achieve true *sagesse*: "...La religion et la prud'hommie, la dévotion et la conscience, je les voeux toutes deux jointes en celuy que j'instruis icy...",[29] but religion is not the generalization of all virtues, "...c'est au rebours car la Religion qui est postérieure, est une vertu spéciale et particulière, distincte de toutes les autres vertus".[30]

Now where did Charron go to find the kind of material suitable for his purpose? Like Montaigne and the other moralists of the time Charron, following the good humanist tradition, dipped into the works of the ancients, familiar to him since his earliest school years. Again like Montaigne —and Charron admits it— from time to time he borrowed from modern treatises pertinent to the subject, using the same words and form, "ne le pouvant dire mieux qu'eux".[31]

This is where Montaigne and Charron resemble one other, as they may resemble some of their contemporaries: both were subjected to the same environment, and both were men of their own epoch who rose high enough above the often crazed and frenzied crowd of their contemporaries to lend these crowds moral support and to offer them intellectual leadership.

Charron's leadership happened to be the more positive and constructive of the two, and this is why for a while the *Sagesse* was more popular than the *Essays*. In the bitter atmosphere where both sides had accumulated hatreds and grievances which lasted for decades to come, many open and moderate minds on both the Protestant and Catholic sides must have tired of hearing discussions in which the doctors of opposite sides always claimed to be right, and of witnessing conversions where politics, violence, or interest had more weight than sincerity. They had a longing for a *terrain d'entente* where they could reconcile anew their ideals and their faith. Montaigne offered them his *Essays*, but they had not been educated in the writings of the ancients like Montaigne, and they

---

28 *Ibid.*, p. 396.
29 *Ibid.*, p. 397.
30 *Ibid.*, p. 399.
31 Charron, *Sagesse*, 1607, p. 748.

could not readily digest his humanism. Montaigne was too modern for them; they did not yet speak his language. Although Charron received the same formal humanistic education, he spoke a language that his contemporaries understood. They had listened to his sermons for many years, and he knew how to hold their attention.

It is here that one sees the greatness and the importance of Charron. In 1595, after the second edition of the *Trois Vérités* had been published, our preacher stepped down from the pulpit and offered his *De la Sagesse* as *terrain d'entente* to his contemporaries. He wrote it as he did his sermons, analysing and carefully weighing each step. The new generation, humanistic in spirit but still under the spell of medieval rhetoric, clamored so loudly for the *De la Sagesse* that from 1601 to 1630 the *Sagesse* went through more editions than the *Essais*. From 1618 to 1634, only sixteen years during the pre-classic period, there were thirteen different editions of the *Sagesse*,[33] and by 1672 it had gone through at least thirty-nine editions. For more than thirty years after his death our canon remained as famous for his writings as he had been during his life for his sermons. Within a few years Charron's influence was being felt in England, and particularly by the English poet William Drummond.[34]

Since the beginning of the twentieth century Charron has received more and more attention in studies of rationalism and of religious thought in seventeenth-century France. Sometimes he has received attention second only to Montaigne, or sometimes even an entire book has been devoted to him, as is the case with Sabrié. But the old *esprit de Sorbonne* is not dead, and we have seen how L'Abbé Brémond, using a style which Garasse himself would have envied, castigated Sabrié for daring to give too much importance to Charron and his *Sagesse*.

In conclusion, I believe that I have established that Charron is anything but "a disciple of Montaigne". As a churchman, celebrated for his sermons and appreciated by his superiors, he achieved great

---

[32] *Mémoires-Journaux*, Pierre de l'Estoile describes so well in his *Mémoires-Journaux* how easily it could be influenced by certain *prédicateurs á la mode*; see also supra, p. 52.

[33] Sabrié, *op. cit.*, p. 494. We have listed fiftyone different editions of the *Sagesse*, infra pp. 147 ff.

[34] William Drummond of Hawthornden, *The Poetical Works*, by L. E. Kastner, Manchester: The University Press, 1913. Mr. Kastner, in his study of Drummond's imitative proclivities, shows that in his prose essay. "A Cypress Grove", the poet is much indebted to the *Sagesse*.

recognition for his performances in the highly responsible tasks with which he was entrusted; as a thinker and a philosopher he exerted on his generation, and the one that followed, a much more positive influence than did the author of the *Essays,* and he diverted the energy of humanism toward the rationalism which is basic to the progress of our modern age.

Unfortunate misinterpretations of his work, initiated by prejudiced critics who wanted to discredit him, have placed him in an unfavorable light as an "imitator of Montaigne". In arguing against this concept and in attempting to give a new and truer picture of our canon I believe that I have laid the foundation for a more accurate understanding of the role of Charron in the history of his age.

BIBLIOGRAPHY

EDITIONS OF THE WORKS ON CHARRON

The starred items are those we were able to obtain and consult; the letter "U" means that the edition is unauthorized

Les Trois Vérités

Charron, Pierre. *Les Trois Véritez Contre les Athées, Idolatres, Juifs, Mahumetans, Hérétiques, & Schismatiques.* Bourdeaus: S. Millanges, 1593.

U———. *Les Trois Véritez Contre tous Athées, Idolatres, Juifs, Mahumetans, Hérétiques, & Schismatiques.* Paris: Leger Delas, 1594.

*———. *Les Trois Véritez Seconde Edition Reveuë, Corrigée & de Beaucoup Augmentée, Avec un Advertissement & Bref Examen, sur la Response Faicte à la Troisieme Vérité, de Nouveau Imprimée à La Rochelle.* Bourdeaux: S. Millanges, 1595.

U———. *Les Trois Véritez Contre tous Athées, Idolatrés, Juifs, Mahumétans, Héritiques, et Schismatiques. Le tout traicté en trois livres.* Paris: Jean du Carroy, 1595.

U———. *Les Trois Véritez Contre les Athées, Idolatres, Juifs, Mahumétans, Héritiques, èt Schismatiques. Le tout traicté en trois livres.* Par M. Benoist Vaillant [sic], Advocat de Sainte Foy. Bruxelles: Rutger Velpius, 1595.

U———. *La Replique de Maistre Pierre le Charron, sur la Response Faicte à sa troisiesme vérité cy devant Imprimée à la Rochelle.* Paris: Estienne Vallet, 1595.

U———. *La Replique de Maistre Pierre le Charron, sur la Résponce faite à sa troisiesme Vérité cy devant imprimée à la Rochelle.* Lyon: Jean Didier, 1695 [sic for 1595].

U*———. *Les Trois Veritez contre tous Athées, Idolatres, Juifs, Mahumetans, Hérétiques, & Schismatiques. Le tout traicté en trois livres.* Lyon: Jean Didier, 1596.

U———. *La Replique de Maistre Pierre lè Charron, sur la Responce faite à la troisiesme Vérité cy devant imprimée à la Rochelle.* Lyon: Jean Didier, 1596.

———. *Les Trois Véritez.* Paris: Veuve Bertault, 1620.

———. *La Replique de Maistre Jean le Charron* [*sic*] *sur la Responce faite à sa troisiesme Verité.* París: Veuve Bertault.

———. *La Verité troisiesme, De toutes lès parts qui sont en la Chrestienté, la Catholique Romaine est la meilleure, contre tous Hérétiques & Schismatiques.* Paris: Robert Bartault, 1623.

Charron, Pierre. *Les Trois Véritez trosiesme edition, reveue, corrigée, et de beaucoup augmentée, plus augmentée de la replique faicte aux Ministres de la Rochelle.* Paris: Robert Bertault, 1625.

———. *La Replique de Maistre Jean le Charron* [*sic*] *sur la Response faicte à la III. Verité, cy-devant Imprimée à la Rochelle.* Paris: Robert Bertault, 1625.

Discours Chrétiens

*Charron, Pierre. *L'Octave Contenant Huict Discours du S. Sacrement. Avec un Autre Discours de la Communion des Saincts.* Bourdeaus: S. Millanges, 1600.

———. *Discours Chrestiens. Seconde Partie.* Bourdeaus: S. Millanges, 1601.

*———. *Discours Chrestiens de la Divinité, Creation, Rédemption et Octaves du Sainct Sacrement.* Paris: P. Bertault, 1604.

*———. *Discours Chrestien, Qu'il n'est Permis ny Loisible a un Subject, Pour Quelque Cause & Raison Que ce Soit, de se Liguer, Bander, & Rebeller Contre son Roy.* Paris: D. Le Clerc, 1606.

*———. *Discours Chrestien, Sur la Benediction Donnée par Isaac à Jacob son Fils Puisné, Pensant la Donner à Esaü son Aisné.* Paris: D. Le Clerc, 1606.

———. *Discours Chrestien de la Divinité, Creation, Redemption et Octaves du Sainct Sacrement.* Paris: R. Bertault, 1622.

De la Sagesse

*Charron, Pierre. *De la Sagesse Livres Trois. Par M. Pierre le Charron, Parisien, Chanoine Theologal & Chantre en l'Eglise Cathedrale de Comdom.* Bourdeaus, S. Millanges, 1601.

———. *De la Sagesse Trois Livres. Par Pierre Charron Parisien Docteur es Droicts. Seconde édition reveuë et Augmentée.* Paris: D. Douceur, 1604.

———. *De la Sagesse Livres Trois. Par M. Pierre le Charron, Parisien, Chanoine Theologal & Chantre en l'Eglise Cathédrale de Comdom. Jouxte la Coppie Imprimée à Bourdeaux.* Bordeaux: S. Millanges, 1606, pp. 734.

———. *De la Sagesse Livres Trois. Par M. Pierre le Charron, Parisien, Chanoine Theologal & Chantre en l'Eglise Cathédrale de Comdom. Jouxte la Coppie Imprimée a Bourdeaux.* Bordeaux: S. Millanges, 1606, pp. 776.

U———. *Le Thrésor de la Sagesse compris en trois livres par M. Pierre Le Charron, Parisien.* Lyon: François le Fèvre, 1606.

*———. *De la Sagesse Trois Livres, Par Pierre Charron Parisien, Docteur és Droicts. Dernière edition, En laquelle, Pour le Contentement du Curieux Lecteur, a Esté adjousté à la Fin Tout ce qui Pouvoit Avoir Esté Retranché aux Precedentes Impressions. Plus un "Eloge" Véritable, ou Sommaire de la Vie de l'Autheur, l'Explication de la Figure qui est au Frontispice du Present Livre, Avec une Table des Matières Principales y Contenues.* 1 vol., Paris: David Douceur, 1607.

———. *De la Sagesse, Par Pierre Charron Parisien.* 2 vols., Paris: David Douceur, 1607.

Charron, Pierre. *De la Sagesse Livres Trois. Jouxte la Coppie Imprimée à Bourdeaux.* Bourdeaux: S. Millanges, 1611.

———. *De la Sagesse Trois Livres. Ausquels est Adjousté un Recueil des Lieux & Chapitres, Suivant la Première Edition de Bordeaux, 1601.* Paris: D. Douceur, 1613.

———. *De la Sagesse, Troisiesme Édition Reveue et Augmentée.* Paris: D. Douceur, 1614.

———. *De la Sagesse.* Rouen: L. Costé, 1614.

———. *De la Sagesse.* Rouen: F. Daré, 1614.

———. *De la Sagesse. Dernière édition.* Rouen: C. le Villain, 1618.

———. *De la Sagesse. Dernière édition.* Rouen: Vernel, 1618.

———. *De la Sagesse.* Paris: J. Meiat, 1621.

———. *De la Sagesse.* Paris: R. Feugé, 1621.

———. *De la Sagesse.* Paris: R. Feugé, 1622.

———. *De la Sagesse.* Rouen: D. Cousturier, 1623.

———. *De la Sagesse.* Rouen: C. Le Villain, 1623.

———. *De la Sagesse.* Rouen: L. Laudet, 1623.

———. *De la Sagesse.* Paris: J. Bessin, 1628.

———. *De la Sagesse.* Paris: R. Fugé [sic], 1630.

———. *De la Sagesse.* Paris: R. Fugé [sic], 1632.

———. *De la Sagesse.* Paris: L. Laudet, 1634.

———. *De la Sagesse.* Rouen: R. Valentin, 1634.

———. *De la Sagesse.* Paris: R. Feugé, 1640.

———. *De la Sagesse.* Paris: R. Fugé [sic], 1646.

———. *De la Sagesse.* Leide: les Elzeviers, 1646.

———. *De la Sagesse.* Leide: J. Elzevier, 1656.

———. *De la Sagesse.* Paris: Journel, 1657.

———. *De la Sagesse.* Leide: J. Elzevier, 1659.

*———. *De la Sagesse.* Amsterdam: L. et D. Elzevier, 1662. Suivant la Vraye Copie de Bourdeaux.

———. *De la Sagesse.* Paris: J. Le Gras, 1662.

———. *De la Sagesse.* Paris: G. Quinet, 1663.

———. *De la Sagesse.* Paris: J. Le Gras, 1664.

———. *De la Sagesse.* Paris: A. Besoigne, 1671.

———. *De la Sagesse.* Paris: A. Besoigne, 1672.

———. *De la Sagesse suivant la Vraye copie de Bourdeaux pour servir de suite aux Essais de Montaigne.* 2 vols., Paris: Herissant fils, 1768.

———. *De la Sagesse suivant la Vraye copie de Bourdaux pour servir de suite aux Essais de Montaigne.* 2 vols., Londres: 1769.

———. *De la Sagesse.* Genève: P. Cazin, 1777.

———. *De la Sagesse.* Amsterdam: 1782.

———. *De la Sagesse.* Paris: J. Fr. Bastien, 1783.

———. *De la Sagesse.* Paris: Barrois, 1789.

———. *De la Sagesse,* 1 vol., Paris: C. Laigneau, 1797.

———. *De la Sagesse.* 2 vols., Paris: C. Laigneau, 1797.

———. *De la Sagesse, trois livres, Nouvelle Edition.* 4 vols., Dijon: L. N. Frantin, 1801.

*———. *De la Sagesse. Collection des Moralistes Français.* Edited by Amaury Duval. 3 vols., Paris: Chassériau, 1824.

———. *De la Sagesse. Choix de Moralistes Français.* Edited by Jean Buchon. Paris: Panthéon Littéraire, 1835.

Charron, Pierre. *De la Sagesse. Choix de Moralistes Français.* Edited by Jean Buchon. Paris: Panthéon Littéraire, 1843.

———. *De la Sagesse. Choix de Moralistès Français.* Edited by Jean Buchon. Paris: Panthéon Littéraire, 1880.

Traicté de Sagesse

*Charron, Pierre. *Traicté de Sagesse. Plus Quelques Discours Chrestiens du mesme Autheur, qui ont esté Trouvez Apres son Décez Avec son Portraict au Naturel, & l'Eloge ou Sommaire de sa Vie.* Paris: D. le Clerc, 1606.

———. *Traicté de Sagesse. Plus Quelques Discours Chrestiens du Mesme Autheur.* Paris: D. le Clerc, 1608.

———. *Traicté de Sagesse. Plus Quelques Discours Chrestiens du Mesme Autheur.* Paris: M. Durand, 1614.

———. *Traicté de Sagesse.* Paris: J. Bessin, 1618.

———. *Traicté de Sagessė.* Paris: Veuve Méiat, 1621.

———. *Traicté de Sagesse.* Paris: R. Feugé, 1621.

———. *Traicté de Sagesse.* Paris: R. Feugé, 1622.

———. *Traicté de Sagesse.* Rouen: D. Cousturier, 1623.

———. *Traicté de Sagesse.* Rouen: C. Le Villain, 1623.

———. *Traicté de Sagesse.* Paris: R. Feugé, 1629.

———. *Traité de Sagesse.* Paris: R. Feugé, 1632.

———. *Traicté de Sagesse.* Rouen: L. Laudet, 1634.

———. *Traicté de Sagèsse.* Rouen: R. Valentin, 1634.

*———. *Traicté de Sagesse.* Paris: R. Feugé, 1642.

———. *Traicté de Sagesse.* Paris: R. Feugé, 1645.

Toutes Les Oeuvres

*Charron, Pierre. *Toutes Les Oeuvrės de Pierre Charron. Parisien, Docteur es Droicts, Chantre et Chanoinė Théologal de Condom. Dernière édition. Reveues, corrigées & augmentées.* Paris: Jacques Villery, 1635.

Translations and adaptations

*Charron, Pierre. *Of Wisdom. Translated by Samson Lennard.* London: Blount, 1612.

*———. *Of Wisdom.* Edited by Samson Lennard. London: 1658.

———. *Of Wisdom.* Edited by George Stanhope. 1697.

———. *Of Wisdom.* Edited by George Stanhope. 2d ed., 1707.

*———. *Of Wisdom.* Edited by George Stanhope. 3d ed., 1729.

———. *De la Sabiduría.* Buenos Aires: Losada, 1948.

———. *The Right of Kings and duty of subjects. An extract from Dr. Stanhope's translation of the author's celebrated book of Wisdom.* London: (no date).

Roche du Maine, J. P. L. de la, Marquis de Luchet. *Analysė Raisonnée de la Sagesse de Charron.* 2 vols., Amsterdam: 1763.

Charron, Pierre. *Della Savìezza, di Pietro Charron*, libri tre. Venèzia: 1768.

*Roche du Maine, J. P. L. de la, Marquis de Luchet. *Analyse Raisonnée de la Sagesse de Charron*. 2 vols., London: 1789.

Myrtilla, H. *A Treatise of Wisdom by Pierre Charron*. New York: P. Putnam's Sons, 1891.

STUDIES AND CRITICAL MATERIALS ON THE MAN AND HIS WORKS

Adam, Antoine. *Histoire de la Littérature Française Au XVII*^e^ *Siècle*. Paris: Domat, 1948.

Algermissen, Konrad. *Christian Denominations*. Translated by Rev. Joseph W. Grundner. 3d ed., St. Louis: B. Herder Book Co., 1948.

Aubigné, Agrippa (d.). *Histoire Universelle*. By De Ruble. Paris: Renouard, 1892.

Auvray, Louis. "Lettres de Pierre Charron". *Revuė d'Histoire Littéraire de la France*. Vol. I, Paris: Colin, 1894.

Barbier, A. A. *Dictionnaire Des Ouvrages Anonymes*. Paris: Fetchoz & Letouzay, 1882.

Bayle, Pierre. *Dictionnaire Historiquė et Critique*. Vol. IV, La Haye: 1737.

Bonnefon, Paul: *Montaigne et Ses Amis*. 2 vols., Paris: Armand Colin, 1898.

Brémond, Henri. "La Folle 'Sagesse' de Pierre Charron". *Correspondant*. Vol. 252, Juillet, 1913.

———. *Histoire Littéraire du Sentiment Religieux en France Depuis la Fin des Guerres de Religion Jusq'à Nos Jours*. Vol. VII, Paris: Blond et Gay, 1916-1936.

Bruckeri, Jacobi. *Historia Critica Philosophiae a Tempore Resuscitatarum in Occidente Litterorum ad Nostra Tempora*. Vol. IV, Lipsiae: 1742-1744.

Brunet, Jacques Charles. *Manuel du Libraire et de l'Amateur des Livres*. Vol. I, Paris: F. Didot, 1860.

Brunetière, Ferdinand. *Histoire de la Littérature Française Classique. Le XVII*^e^ *Siècle*. Vol. II, Paris: Delagrave, 1912.

Buffier, P. *Cours de Sciences Sur des Principės Nouveaux et Simples Pour Former Le Langage, l'Esprit et le Coeur Dans l'Usage Ordinaire de la Vie*. Paris: 1632.

Busson, Henri. *Les Sources ėt le Développement du Rationalisme Dans la Littérature Française de la Renaissance*. Paris: Letouzey et Ané, 1922.

———. *La Pensée Religieuse Française de Charron à Pascal*. Paris: J. Vrin, 1933.

Charron, Jean. "Pierre Charron as Seen Through His Petit Traicté de Sagesse". Unpublished Master's Thesis, Dept. of Romance Languages, University of North Carolina, 1953.

Cheffonds, Christophe de. *Novae Illustrationis Christianae Fideiadversus Impios, Libertinos, Atheos, Epicureos et Omne Genus Infideles*. Paris: 1586.

Chinard, Gilbert. *L'Exotisme Américain dans la Littérature Française au XVI*^e^ *Siècle*. Paris: Hachette, 1911.

Cousin, Jean. *Fundamenta Religionis, Hoc Est, Tractatus de Naturali Dei Cognitione, de Animi Immortalitate et de Justitia Dei Adversus Politicorum Seu Atheorum Errores.* Duaci, 1597.

Delboulle, A. "Charron Plagiaire de Montaigne". *Revue d'Histoire Littéraire de la France.* Vol. VII, Paris: 1900.

Descartes, René. *Oeuvres Complètes.* Edited by C. Adam and P. Tannery. Paris: L. Cerf, 1897-1910.

Dezeimeris, R. *De la Renaissance des Lettres à Bordeaux au XVI Siècle.* Bordeaux: 1864.

Dréano, Maturin. *La Pensée Religieuse de Montaigne.* Paris: Beauchesne et ses fils, 1936.

Drummond, William, of Hawthornden. *The Poetical Works.* Edited by L. E. Kastner. Manchester: The University Press, 1913.

Eymard, Julien. "Le Stoicisme en France Dans la 1er Moitié du XVIIe Siècle, Pierre Charron, Le Stoicisme Chrétien, Guillaume du Vair". *Etudes Franciscaines.* Vol. II, December, Paris: 1951.

Faguet, Emile. *Histoire de la Littérature Française.* Vol. I, Paris: Plon, 1901.

———. *L'Anticléricalisme.* Paris: 1906.

Guiraud, L. "Le séjour de Pierre Charron à Montpellier, 1565-1569 et 1570-1571". *Bulletin Philologique et Historique,* Paris, 1913.

Hanotaux, Gabriel. *Histoire de la Nation Française.* Vol. IV, *Histoire Politique de 1515 à 1804.* By Louis Madelin. Paris: Plon, 1924.

Hauser, Henri. *Etudes sur la Réforme Française.* Paris: A. Picard, 1909.

Hauser, Henri, and Renaudet, Augustin. *Les Débuts de l'Age Moderne, la Renaissance, et la Réforme.* Paris: 1929.

Hoefer. *Nouvelle Biographie Génerale.* Vol. X, Paris: F. Didot Frères, 1855.

Holmes, Urban T., Lyons, John C., and Linker, Robert W. *Guillaume de Salluste Seigneur du Bartas,* 3 vols., Chapel Hill: University of North Carolina Press, 1935-41.

Imbart, De la Tour. *Les Origines de la Réforme.* 3 vols. Paris: Hachette, 1905-14.

Jal, A. *Dictionnaire Critique de Biographie et d'Histoire.* Paris: H. Plon, 1872.

Joly. *Remarques sur le Dictionnaire de Bayle.* Paris: 1748.

Jurien, Pierre. *Apologie Pour la Réformation Pour les Réformateurs et Pour les Réformez.* Rotterdam: Reinierleers, 1683.

La Ferrière, Hector (de). *Lettres de Catherine de Medici.* Paris: Imprimerie Nationale, 1895.

La Rochemaillet, Gabriel Michel (de). "Eloge" published with *Les Oeuvres Complètes de Pierre Charron.* Paris: Villery, 1635.

Lanson, Gustave. "Pierre Charron". *Grande Encyclopédie.* Edited by H. Lamirault, Vol. X.

Lavisse, Ernest. *Histoire de France.* Vol. VI, *La Réforme et la Ligue.* By Jean H. Mariéjol. Paris: Hachette, 1911.

L'Estoile, Pierre (de). *Mémoires-Journaux.* Paris: Librairie des Bibliophiles, 1880.

Lachèvre, Fréderic. *Le Libertinage au XVIIe Siècle.* 2 vols. Paris: Champion, 1909.

Martin, Henri. *Histoire de France.* Vol. II, Paris: Furne, 1857.

Martin, Victor. *Le Gallicanisme et la Réforme Catholique: Essai Sur l'Introduction en France des Décrets du Concile de Trente (1563-1615).* Paris: Picard, 1919.

Martin, Victor. *Le Gallicanisme Politique et le Clergé de France.* Paris: Picard, 1929.

Michaud. *Biographie Universelle Ancienne et Moderne.* Paris: Delagrave.

Mongredien, George. *La Vie Littéraire au XVIIeme Siècle.* Paris: J. Taillandier, 1947.

Monmerqué, M. *Lettres de Madame de Sévigné.* Vol. IX, Paris: Hachette, 1862.

Montaigne. *Les Essais.* Edited by P. Villey, 3 vols. Paris: Alcan, 1922.

Pascal, Blaise. *Oeuvres Complètes.* Edited by L. Brunschvigg, P. Boutroux, F. Gazier. Paris: Hachette, 1904-1914.

Pintard, René. *Le Libèrtinage Erudit dans la Première Moitié du XVIIeme Siècle.* Paris: Boivin, 1943.

Plattard, Jean. *Une Figure de Premier Plan Dans nos Lettres de la Renaissance, Agrippa d'Aubigné.* Paris: Boivin, 1931.

———. *Montaigne et son Temps.* Paris: Boivin, 1933.

———. *Etat Présent dès Études sur Montaigne.* Paris: Belles-Lettres, 1935.

Reimanni, Jacob F. *Historia Universalis Atheismi et Atheorum Falso et Merito Suspectorum Apus Judaeos, Ethnicos, Christianos, Mahu Metanos Ordine Chronologico Descripta, ab Suis Initiis Usque ad Nostra Tempora Deducta.* Hildesiae: 1725.

Rice, Eugene F. Jr. *The Renaissance Idea of Wisdom.* (Harvard Historical Monographs, XXXVII.) Cambridge, Mass.: Harvard University Press, 1958.

Roeder, Ralph. *Catherine de Medici and the Lost Revolution.* New York: The Viking Press, 1937.

Rousseau, J. J.: *Oeuvres Complètes.* 8 vols. Paris: 1858.

Sabrié, J. B. *Dė l'Humanisme au Rationalisme, Pierre Charron (1541-1603), l'Homme, l'Oeuvre, l'Influence.* Paris: Alcan, 1913.

Sainte-Beuve, C. A. *Causeries du Lundi.* Vol. IV, Paris: Garnier Frères, 1868.

———. *Les Grands Écrivains Français. Études des Lundis.* Vol. III, Paris: Garnier Fréres, 1926.

———. *Port Royal.* Vol. I, Paris: Hachette, 1901.

Sorel, M. C. *La Bibliothèque Française de M. C. Sorel ou le Choix et l'Examen des Livres François Qui Traitent de l'Éloquence de la Philosophie, de la Dévotion ėt de la Conduite des Moeurs.* Paris: La Compagnie des Libraires du Palais, 1664.

Strowski, Fortunat. *Histoire du Sentiment Religieux en France au XVIIe Siècle, Pascal et Son Temps, Ier Partie, De Montaignė à Pascal.* Paris: Plon, 1909.

———. *Montaigne.* Paris: Editions de la Nouvelle Revue Critique, 1938.

Tilley, Arthur. *From Montaigne to Molière.* Cambridge, England: The University Press, 1923.

Villey, Pierre. *Les Sources et l'Evolution des Essais de Montaigne.* 2 vols. Paris: Hachette, 1908.

———. *Les Sources d'Idées au XVIe Siècle.* Paris: Plon, 1912.

Zyromski, Ernest. *L'Orgueil Humain.* Paris: Armand Colin, 1904.

www.ingramcontent.com/pod-product-compliance
Lightning Source LLC
LaVergne TN
LVHW090957080826
845145LV00003B/1041

* 9 7 8 0 8 0 7 8 9 0 3 4 9 *